PLAY REDUX

DIGITALCULTUREBOOKS is an imprint of the University of Michigan Press and the Scholarly Publishing Office of the University of Michigan Library dedicated to publishing innovative and accessible work exploring new media and their impact on society, culture, and scholarly communication.

PLAY REDUX

THE FORM OF COMPUTER GAMES

David Myers

THE UNIVERSITY OF MICHIGAN PRESS AND
THE UNIVERSITY OF MICHIGAN LIBRARY
Ann Arbor

Copyright © by the University of Michigan 2010

All rights reserved

Published in the United States of America by

The University of Michigan Press and

The University of Michigan Library

Manufactured in the United States of America

♾ Printed on acid-free paper

2013   2012   2011   2010   4   3   2   1

A CIP catalog record for this book is available from the British Library.

Library of Congress Cataloging-in-Publication Data

Myers, David.

  Play redux : the form of computer games / David Myers.

    p.   cm.

  Includes bibliographical references and index.

  ISBN 978-0-472-07092-3 (cloth : alk. paper) — ISBN 978-0-472-05092-5
(pbk. : alk. paper)

  1. Computer games—Social aspects. 2. Play—Social aspects.
I. Title.

GV1469.17.S63M95   2010

  794.8—dc22   2009038405

God bless everyone.
Mother and Daddy.
Nanee and GeeGee.
Grandma and Grandpa.
Kim.
Me.
Megan and Sarah.
Susan.
And all the rest.
Play ball.

CONTENTS

Introduction

Play is a very interesting thing. Somewhat strangely, though, play is not studied as often as are the consequences of play.

The reason for this becomes clear when we try to study play: it is a very hard thing to study. Play resists our scrutiny in characteristically slippery ways. One of these is the degree to which play is dependent on and determined by *paradox*. In *The Nature of Computer Games* (2003), I spent a great deal of time focusing on the paradoxical nature of play. In that book, I classified paradoxes according to commonly accepted categories, examined common features of those categories, and concluded that paradoxes—and most particularly play-related paradoxes—are a form of self-reference.

Prototypical examples of self-referential paradoxes are these:

- **The Liar's Paradox:** This statement is false.
- **Russell's Paradox:** The set of all sets that are not members of themselves.

In the Liar's Paradox, the "statement" refers to itself directly; in Russell's Paradox, the "set" refers to itself by including itself in its own membership. The result, in both cases, is that we have trouble understanding what these paradoxes *mean*. When we try to derive a meaning from the Liar's Paradox, for instance, we find our meaning-making process oscillating between thinking the statement is true (which it must be in order to be false) and thinking the statement is false (because, after all, that is what the statement says it is).

This oscillation of meaning doesn't stop. And because we find ourselves (potentially forever) in the midst of this oscillation, befuddled, our awareness and attention turn from the meaning we cannot derive to the meaning-making process that cannot derive it. That is, we turn our awareness and attention from the *content* of meaning to the *form* of meaning (and/or the lack thereof).

In this brief analysis, then, are a couple of important realizations concerning the nature and study of play that I wish to pursue further here. First and foremost, play involves a special form of self-reference. And because play exhibits a particular self-referential *form*—similar to paradox—the study of play offers opportunities for formalist methods of study. Second, a self-referential form is also, obviously and importantly, referential. Therefore, the study of play should involve not only the study of self-referential forms but also the study of references and referencing in general: that is, semiosis.

Currently and curiously, the study of play does not often focus on either its formal properties or its semiotic properties as much as it focuses on other things. The most prominent and frequent of these other things is culture.

In the 1970s, which was quite some time ago it seems, I was an undergraduate English major at Yale University. Walking across campus on some dark and snowy eve, a fellow student pointed out to me a bearish figure receding in the distance, coated and capped, who was, I was told, William K. Wimsatt, "the formalist."

After a long career in academia, Wimsatt died in 1975; his primary teaching duties at Yale had been curtailed—if not completed entirely—sometime before that. Thus, I am uncertain whether this figure in memory was Wimsatt indeed or simply one relatively naive student's wild speculation to another. In any case, that particular image has stuck in my mind as emblematic of the decline of formalists and formalism, both of which were, by the mid-1970s, being shunted into obscurity.

During the mid-twentieth century and beyond, formalist models of literature were superseded by structuralist models of history and, subsequently buoyed by post-structuralism, cultural studies. In this supersession, cultural studies relegated the study of language and literature—and aesthetics in general—to a subset of its own broader, more inclusive, and often impenetrably complex view of social relationships as instrumental and unavoidable in determining human thoughts, interpretations, and meanings.

Ostensibly, semiotics is the study of semiosis, or the human meaning-making process. However, in common practice, semiotics as an academic discipline has tended to adopt a particular set of assumptions regarding how and under what influences a human-like meaning-making process operates. These assumptions are, by and large, equivalent to those of cultural studies. Thus, conventional semiotic analysis situates the human meaning-making process in a particular cultural context.

This is contrary to the assumptions I am going to bring to bear here, and it is contrary to the original assumptions of formalism as held and promoted by William K. Wimsatt, Cleanth Brooks, Viktor Shklovsky, and other similar formalists.

Wimsatt and Beardsley (1954) coined the terms *intentional fallacy* and *affective fallacy* to emphasize exactly this issue. The tenets of their "New Criticism" claimed that it is the literary work itself—its interior mechanics—that determine its value as literature, or its "literariness." If you were, rather, to determine that literariness on the basis of author intent—including author history, culture, or psychology—then you would be guilty of an "intentional fallacy." Likewise, if you were, rather, to determine that literariness on the basis of audience (reader) response—emotive or otherwise—you would suffer from an "affective fallacy."

Above all other things, it is this claim that sets formalism apart from its opposition: the formal properties of an artwork are its defining properties.

When we apply an unadulterated formalism to the study of play, we produce a similar claim: the formal properties of play are the defining properties of that play. This is the primary claim I will make here, and this claim (if true) allows us to position semiotics, in contrast to its position within cultural studies, as a *science*. At its core, semiotics as a science investigates representationalism, intentionality, and human meaning-making as fundamental components of human activity and expression and, equally importantly, as more general features of the natural world. For, although human meaning-making processes often behave and feel as though they were subjective, semiotics as a science would attempt to uncover their objective properties, regardless of cultural context. These objective properties may appear most evident in the mechanics of a common, singular, and universal meaning-making *form*.

The most oft-cited studies of play and the historical basis for most contemporary play and game studies are not formalist studies. The two most prominent of these are Huizinga's *Homo Ludens* (1938) and Caillois' *Man, Play, and Games* (1961). Each of these early works has something important to say regarding the crucial issue of whether human culture is determinant of or determinable by human play.

Huizinga's thesis, for instance, is clear:

The aim . . . is to integrate the concept of play into that of culture. Consequently, play is . . . understood . . . not as a biological phenomenon but as a cultural phenomenon.[1]

Yet Huizinga's analysis subsequently reveals play as dependent on something other than cultural contingency.

> If this innate tendency of the mind . . . is in fact rooted in play, then we are confronted with a very serious issue. We can only touch on it here. The play attitude must have been present before human culture or human speech existed.[2]

Caillois' book, more focused and restrictive in theme than that of Huizinga, prefers to examine and categorize toys and games ("the residues of culture," p. 58) rather than either play or culture in broader contexts. To this end, Caillois' analysis is largely directed toward attempting to uncover—the same attempt I will make here—universal properties of play as form: "These diverse qualities [of play activities] are purely formal. They do not prejudge the content of games" (p. 10).

Thus, both Huizinga and Caillois (much more readily, in fact, than most contemporary analyses of computer games) acknowledge a cross-cultural and interdisciplinary play element: an element that is formal, biological, and, ultimately, universal.

The consensual successor to the early Huizinga and Caillois landmark studies is Sutton-Smith's well-received *The Ambiguity of Play* (2001). This book is the crowning achievement of one of the most prolific, influential, and insightful scholars of play in the latter half of the twentieth century; yet *The Ambiguity of Play* is also quite characteristic of the current "cultural turn."[3]

In *The Ambiguity of Play*, as the title implies, Sutton-Smith describes seven distinct play "rhetorics," each indicative of a particular set of cultural values and beliefs. It is only in the final chapters of his book that Sutton-Smith, almost reluctantly, offers his own definition of a culturally independent play that he describes as "adaptive variability."

> Evolution is characterized by quirky shifts and latent potential. What could be more fundamental in talking about all forms of play than to describe them in terms of the centrality of this notion of quirky shifts? . . . The notion that play itself is some kind of adaptive variability, and therefore presumably some kind of reinforcement of realistic adaptive variability, is very attractive.[4]

> I define play as a facsimilization of the struggle for survival.[5]

Despite claims such as these (which I find very attractive as well), Sutton-Smith, in the current fashion, qualifies his biologically derived definition with reference to some larger cultural context in which it must reside: "Despite my extensive criticism of the rhetoric of progression, I have now invented yet another form of it" (p. 231).

I will not attempt hereafter, as Sutton-Smith has, to allay the concerns of cultural studies; I will attempt to more directly assert the assumptions and consequences of a biologically derived human play that is most recognizable in its common formal properties. Huizinga, Caillois, Sutton-Smith, and others have referenced these properties, but always without embracing—or confronting—them fully. These unrealized assumptions within the cultural studies of play might be least controversially labeled *biological naturalism*, which supposes material and objective properties of human cognition as essential to an understanding and analysis of that cognition and, by extension, cognitive play.

Using the assumptions of biological naturalism, I hope to revisit and, hopefully, revitalize formalist aesthetics theories that have been pushed aside in the intervening decades of scholarship since their origin.

The realm of computer games seems an especially good place to attempt this pro-formalist task. For computer games, of all types of games and play, are most securely situated in the formal properties of a digital game *code*, which is much more measurable and more determinable than that code's pre-digital analog: game *rules*.

From the perspective of semiotics as a science, computer games are most essentially *semiotic machines* that generate and transform meanings through the coded manipulation of signs and symbols. The more accurately we are able to replicate these evocative qualities of computer games, the more likely we are to gain insight into some of the more problematic areas of human representationalism. To this end, the procedural structures of computer game design and play may be considered homologous to the human cognitive structures that enable them. Therein, the study of computer game forms and rules—and particularly the study of the interactive and transformative properties of paradoxical play with those rules—has the potential to emulate the representational qualities of the human mind in form and, perhaps, in function.

Admittedly, however, neither computer games nor computer game rules entirely encompass the phenomenon of play; and, in fact, the study of play is well justified in and of itself, with or without special reference to computer games. I have had some occasion to reflect on this larger matter: why the study of play is, in itself, important.

In one instance, David Crookall, the energetic editor of the long-running scholarly journal *Simulation & Gaming*, compiled a reflective issue, to which I contributed. Similarly articulate and energetic editors have called upon me to contribute my thoughts on the value of studying play and games during the initial publication of the relatively new Sage journal *Games and Culture*. The same question was asked in each instance: why do we now have an increasing number of game studies, scholars, journals, and interests?

There is no doubt that much of the current (twenty-first-century) academic interest in computer games and game studies is driven by the recent commercial success of the video game industry. There was, in fact, a brief, but otherwise similar, surge in academic interest in computer games and gaming during the early 1980s; when Atari was in its heyday, Chris Crawford's *Balance of Power* received coverage in the *New York Times Magazine* (Aaron 1985), and I published my first analyses of computer games (Myers 1984).

That early video game market went bust, however, and game scholars went back to what they had been previously doing: designing, playing, and writing about games in a relatively more obscure and less convivial environment. Now, more than twenty years later, as the game industry re-asserts prices and profit margins, we once again find games and the scholarly study of games popular and, increasingly, popularized. Once again, games are interesting and appealing things—as is game *play*.

So, the more important question is not really "Why game studies *now*?" but, rather, "Why game studies *at all*?" Out of several reasons I have given in the past, let me re-emphasize two.

First, the study of games involves the study of play.

In 1999, after reviewing thirty years of articles in *Simulation & Gaming*, I said this:

> What I've found in my review of [*Simulation & Gaming*] is encouraging: the continued and resolute focus on the game-playing *process*. Perhaps this is more by luck than design. Many contributors seem to be either dedicated game designers or game players—or both. It's natural and expected, then, that much of their analysis is based on either game design or play. But, if this is luck, then it's also serendipidity, for (once again) it is exactly the process of play—aside from its effects—that is at the center of the whirlpool of theory in other fields.[6]

After all, what other aspects of human behavior (other than play) are so common, so universal, so pervasive, so profound, and so critical to an understanding of human nature, well-being, and self-consciousness—yet studied so seldom?

Often, play studies are deemed synonymous with child development studies; and too often, theories of play remain narrowly focused within developmental models that, for all their insights, fail to consider seriously the implications of widespread and common adult play. Yet play is surely not so characteristic of the human child as it is of the human species.

Past and current game studies clearly demonstrate that game play is a cross-generational phenomenon. Indeed, definitions of games, based on very curious and sometimes paradoxical distinctions between rules-bound and rules-free systems (see Klabbers 1996), portend revision and transformation of conventional understanding of rules-based systems of all sorts: governments, economies, cultures. Sutton-Smith, in particular, has been influential in extending the study of play beyond the boundaries of child education and development by emphasizing aspects of games and play—rough and "dark" play, for instance—that have been discounted by developmental theorists.

Second, the study of games involves the study of representations.

The study of representations and the study of play are closely connected. The study of representations within games emphasizes formal properties of games; the study of play emphasizes the functional properties of those same aesthetic forms. One of the more intriguing potentials of game studies is to illuminate this connection and, in the process, perhaps resolve some of the more vexing problems in representationalism and philosophy of mind. Prominent among these is what Harnard (1990) terms the "symbol grounding" problem: an information processing dilemma based on the paradoxical implications of an endlessly recursive semiotic process operating without a clear and common reference—or "ground"—to some objective correlative or "other."

In fact, it has long been my contention that problems and anomalies associated with human semiosis—such as the symbol grounding problem—do not result from flaws of thought or logic but, rather, are necessary and inevitable characteristics of representationalism. Game studies may well help specify such problems more clearly—as well as come to some deeper and more complete understanding of the incorrigible nature of their, at best, partial solutions.

Games, like literature, use conventional signs and symbols in unconventional ways. Early formalists focused the study of literature on the nature of "literariness," or on those fundamental properties of literary form both derivative of and in reference to the habits and conventions of a natural language. In this same sense, what are the fundamental properties of games? What properties of game designs and forms distinguish games from other, more conventional acts and objects of human creation and culture?

Surely, these characteristics involve the form and function of *representations* within games. All games—all play—are, after all, *virtual*. And in our current age of the virtual, games and play occupy central positions.

Yet, while most concede some fundamental role to representationalism in understanding and analyzing games, there has been, to date, little overlap between the study of representational form and the study of game form— much less overlap than in other academic fields involving other aesthetic domains.

Linguists, semioticians, and some in philosophy of mind have most often carried this particular interdisciplinary torch forward. But the intellectual net is, in fact, widespread. Early exemplars of a game-related *cognitive aesthetics* include Jakobson's analysis of metaphor and metonymy (Jakobson & Halle 1956), Levi-Strauss's (1979) study of binary structures in myth and culture, Lakoff and Johnson's (1999, 2003) insight into analogies and the origins of language, Marr's (1982) examination of visual perceptions and cues, and Johnson-Laird's (1983) treatise on mental models. Other studies, thematically similar but slightly closer to the study of games and related entertainment forms, include Bordwell's (1989) essays on film, Csikszentmihalyi's (1991) psychological analysis of flow experiences, Grodal's (2003) investigation of the relationship between games and sensations, and Aarseth's (1997) identification of aporia and epiphany as common and fundamental characteristics of game forms.

Each of these reveals how representational forms function as aesthetic objects during the creation, manipulation, and interpretation of signs and symbols. And each of these studies can be usefully applied within a *cognitive aesthetics* (coordinated with a *biological naturalism*) that would correlate phenomenological experiences—"fun," for instance—with more objective, representational, and, ultimately, cognitive forms. Game studies are posed to emphasize, articulate, and explain such a correlation, much to the benefit of cognitive sciences and cognitive aesthetics.

Some further things are perhaps best said here in the beginning.

While I will pursue a formalist analysis, I will not attempt to be either overly technical or, for that matter, strictly precise in describing forms of play and games. This is not entirely an admission of defeat; it is an admission of inaccuracy. The precise nature of a technical explanation of play consistently eludes us all, and so I have come to believe that this elusive characteristic of play *is* its characteristic form.

In analogy, for instance, there is a paradox known as Berry's Paradox: "The least integer not nameable in fewer than nineteen syllables." In previous analysis, I have, as Berry's Paradox attempts to describe its integer, attempted to describe play as, essentially, indescribable. Since I am able to do that only indirectly and only with analogous references to other, similarly indescribable forms, I will attempt to make those references as palatable and accessible here as possible.

Further, if I wish my analysis to be clear, and if I were to look for guidance in the clarity of my academic colleagues, I would find those colleagues in philosophy to be, pretty much by far, the clearest and most able writers. An important element of this clarity, I've noticed, is that articles and publications in philosophy tend to have fewer references than articles and publications in the social sciences, where game studies largely reside. *Principia Mathematica* is a well-known and prototypical example of this ability of the philosopher to find validity in an extended examination of his own argument rather than in the piecemeal—and often rhetorical—introduction of the abridged arguments of others.

While I am not so brave as to disregard entirely the value of the citation-filled treatise, I confess that I have thought about it. As a result, I hope to present my argument here aided as appropriate but unburdened, if possible, by the sometimes overzealous ritual of citation.

In the game studies community, controversies arise, from time to time, concerning the nature and relevance of the examples used to discuss the fundamentals of computer game play. Because the computer game industry, like other digital media industries, undergoes rapid evolution and change, examples of computer games used as a basis for theory development may sometimes be considered too "old" and therein not fully descriptive of more current behavior in computer game play. I rather think, in general, that the opposite is true.

As I argued in *The Nature of Computer Games*, computer game play and design very quickly converged in the 1970s and 1980s into a relatively limited number of still easily recognizable genres and patterns of play. These formal patterns are determined by the relatively intractable nature of human cognition and, thus, are actually often more evident in the simpler and less embellished forms of early computer games than in their later, slicker, and more commercially institutionalized forms.

A related issue here involves the concern that to understand computer game play, it is necessary to fully experience that play. I sympathize strongly with this concern—which poses a serious obstacle for the analysis of a phenomenon that requires, quite literally, hundreds and hundreds of hours of computer game play in order to most intimately learn and understand the systemic nature and individual consequences of computer game play.

Nevertheless, the nature and necessity of computer game play can only be gauged when that play takes place over an extended period of time, in a repetitive and recursive process. That is, the process of play only becomes most evident when and where there are multiple applications of that process.

These multiple applications might take place within a large group of players, or, equally validly, these multiple applications might take place within some single and extended period of play. Therefore, in most cases, here and elsewhere, I have tended to use *expert* computer game play as an indication of what is most likely to occur when computer games are played regularly and extensively. Expert play is better used for this purpose than beginner play in that expert play is more *complete* in its exploration and realization of computer game form.

Finally, a last word on biological naturalism and media determinism: if I wish to position play as originating in the natural history of the human species, then, obviously, the environment in which that species has evolved is important to acknowledge. This synergy between human environment and human behavior is readily apparent in natural affordances—of which computer games make much and significant use.

Computer games—as well as the digital medium they represent—can be considered an environmental influence on human behavior and, one might suspect, therein capable of radically transforming those (like us) who increasingly live, breathe, think, and evolve within a digital landscape. This was indeed the assumption of the once-popular media determinist Marshall McLuhan, who quite literally believed that digital media extended the human senses and, in that process, transformed human cognition. That will not be my position, however.

The most basic argument asserting the primacy of biological code over digital code in determining human behavior is simply this: Given two systems of code, one in human cognition and one in digital media, which could be expected to interact with and, over time, adapt to the other? Which would most likely display the greatest amount of variation and adaptive change over time?

Obviously, it seems to me, the system that is more flexible and capable of change will adapt more quickly and more radically to its environment than will the system that is less flexible and less capable of change. Thus, the code associated with digital media forms is more likely to adapt to the code associated with human interpretive processes—rather than vice versa.[7]

Giving at least face validity to these assumptions, the same simple argument can also be applied to social and cultural "codes." These, too, seem more obviously amenable to sudden change and variation than do biological codes governing human cognitive behavior. Thus, according to the same logic as above, social and cultural rules and systems are more likely to reflect adaptations to human cognitive properties than vice versa.

So, in sum, despite their potential to wreak havoc elsewhere, it is highly unlikely that digital media have had any impact whatsoever on the fundamental properties of human cognition.

Consciousness is a biological process like digestion, photosynthesis, or the secretion of bile. Of course, our conscious lives are shaped by our culture, but culture is itself an expression of our underlying biological capacities.[8]

It is improbable that our species evolved complex adaptations to even agriculture, let alone to postindustrial society . . . The available evidence strongly supports this view of a single, universal, panhuman design, stemming from our long-enduring existence as hunter-gatherers.[9]

In fact, almost without exception, new media technologies have already evolved in accordance with the requirements and characteristics of human sensibilities—rather than vice versa. The evolution of computer games demonstrates this as well as any other new media form: from black and white to color, from flat to three-dimensional visual displays, from mono to surround sound, and from isolated and single-player games to more socially oriented and complex massively multiplayer online role-playing games (MMORPGs—or, for short, MMOs).

And yet, because computer game forms adapt to and model human sensibilities, it does not necessarily follow that computer game play either extends or transforms those sensibilities. Indeed,

it is important to recognize that behavior generated by mechanisms that are adaptations to an ancient way of life are not necessarily adaptive in the modern world.[10]

In other words, self-reflective computer game code does not entail self-enlightening computer game play. One of the enduring themes I wish to promote here is that computer games evolve toward the subjective and the psychophysical and, in that evolution, remain steadfastly apart from the objective, the physical, and the *real*. The consequences of this include self-pleasure and self-understanding, in many cases of computer game play, but also self-delusion, in many others.

Here is what you will find in the rest of the book:

Chapters 1–5 (*What computer games are*) develop a computer game aesthetic, which I position as an *anti-aesthetic*. The first chapter is a description of the fundamentals of play as a semiotic process. Here I establish a model of play as a rules-breaking mechanism and outline critical distinctions, based on this model, among play, games, and simulations.

In Chapter 2, I dwell on the concept of *anti-ness* in form, in philosophy, and, most relevantly, in play.

Chapter 3 establishes some revealing connections between a formal analysis of computer games and play and previous formal analyses of literature and "literariness."

Chapter 4 examines the form of computer games in more detail, highlighting differences between computer game *code* and computer game *interface*, both of which have significant influence during computer game play. This chapter also defines and gives examples of two most important formal properties of computer game play, which together constitute *interactivity:* recursion and contextualization.

In Chapter 5, I summarize the meaning and implications of a computer game *anti-aesthetic* as regards computer game play and existing theories of computer game play, particularly theories based on the assumptions of cultural studies.

Chapters 6–8 (*What computer games aren't*) introduce a more focused analysis of specific computer games in terms of their narrative potentials and the inconsequential nature of those potentials. Chapter 6 debunks the notion of narrative as an important influence on computer game play in general. Chapter 7 looks at the misguided use of narrative-based analysis to understand genres in computer game play, and chapter 8 looks at the presence (infrequent) and absence (often) of narrative influences in Sid Meier's famed *Civilization* computer game series.

Chapters 9–11 (*The self and the social*) deal with one of the more currently engaging topics in game studies: social play. This analysis is most generic in chapter 9 and then increasingly specific and detailed in chapters

10 and 11, regarding the mechanics and consequences of play in the MMO *City of Heroes/City of Villains* (*CoH/V*) (Cryptic Studios, 2004). Chapter 11 describes a case study of *CoH/V* play in which social play and game code are in significant conflict.

Chapter 12 (*The genie in the bottle*), in finale, is quite short. This chapter repeats and re-emphasizes the basic characteristics of computer game play that I have found enlightening elsewhere, as well as making some speculative comments concerning the future of social media and the consequences of social policies directed at regulating and controlling individual and idiosyncratic (e.g., "bad") play in social media contexts.

These chapters are a compilation—not in any particularly ordered sequence, but nevertheless in significant bulk—of a series of similarly themed articles I have presented and published in various game-related conventions and contexts since *The Nature of Computer Games* appeared in 2003. I am grateful to those in charge of such things for allowing the words and ideas of the following original articles to reappear as necessary and appropriate here:

"Forms of rules of games of forms." In J. Sorge & J. Venus, eds., *Erzählformen im computerspiel: Zur medienmorphologie digitaler spiele.* Bielefield: Transcript. 2009.

Play and punishment: The sad and curious case of Twixt. In *The [Player] Conference proceedings.* Copenhagen: IT University of Copenhagen, 2008.

The videogame aesthetic: Play as form. In Mark Wolf & Bernard Perron, eds., *Videogame reader II,* 45–63. New York: Routledge, 2008. Copyright © 2008 from "VIDEO GAME THEORY READER/2/2 by David Myers. Reproduced by permission of Taylor and Francis Group, LLC, a division of Informa plc.

Self and selfishness in online social play. In Akira Baba, ed., *Situated play, Digital Games Research Association Conference proceedings,* 226–34. Tokyo: University of Tokyo, 2007.

Plays of destruction. In B. Perron, ed., *Intermédialités,* 9. 2007.

Video games: Issues in research and learning. *Simulation & Gaming* 36 (2005): 442–46.

Bombs, barbarians, and backstories: Meaning-making within Sid Meier's *Civilization.* In M. Bittanti, ed., *Civilization: Virtual history, real fantasies.* Milan, Italy: Costa & Nolan, 2005.

What's good about bad play? In Y. Pisan, ed., *IEC2005 Conference proceedings.* Sydney, Australia: University of Technology, 2005.

The aesthetics of the anti-aesthetics. In R. Klevjer, ed., *Aesthetics of Play Conference proceedings*. Online. http://www.aesthetics of play. org/myers.php.

Signs, symbols, games, and play. *Games and Culture* 1 (2005): 47–51.

/hide: The aesthetics of group and solo play. In *Changing views: Worlds in Play, Digital Games Research Association Conference proceedings*. CD-ROM. Vancouver, British Columbia, 2005.

Comments on media aesthetics and media policy. Discussion paper presented at State of Play II: Reloaded, New York Law School, New York, October 28–30, 2004.

The anti-poetic: Interactivity, immersion, and other semiotic functions of digital play. In A. Clarke, ed., *COSIGN 2004 Conference proceedings*. Split, Croatia: Art Academy, University of Split, 2004.

The attack of the backstories (and why they won't win). In M. Copier & J. Raessens, eds., *Level up: Digital Games Research Conference proceedings*. CD-ROM. Utrecht: University of Utrecht, 2003.

CHAPTER 1

Bad Play

You wanna play rough?
Okay. Say hello to my little friend.

—Tony Montana, *Scarface* (1983)

There are many encouraging things about the rise of game studies over the past couple of decades, but there are many discouraging things as well. One of the most discouraging is the degree to which the youngish field of game studies has gained credibility by reproducing existing research methodologies and assumptions. Since game studies involves the study of play and since play incorrigibly approaches all objects and topics in an abject state of disbelief and doubt—that is, in a state of *play*—it might be hoped that young game studies scholars, of all their academic colleagues, might display a similar attitude of skepticism, doubt, and disbelief that would lead them, at least in their very own and brand-new field of study, to question the values and beliefs of their academic mentors.

But, no. Computer game studies have quickly become, like all other forms of academic scholarship, very much like all other forms of academic scholarship: *serious.* And imbedded in this seriousness of method (not so bad in and of itself) is a set of seriously debilitating values.

While theories of play and games are generally regarded as serious and therein good, play itself is most often regarded otherwise. Play is notorious in that it is most frequently non-serious and therein *bad*—ignorant, destructive, and/or illegal.

In computer game play, ignorant play is often denigrated as "noob" play; destructive play would include "griefing" and the like; and illegal play in game contexts involves, among other things, exploitation of game rules and codes (including commercial rules) during pirating and hacking activities.

But bad play is obviously a much larger category than just that associated with computer game play. The theoretical term for this bad play is often *dysfunctional play*, and most existing play theory has a hard time explaining why dysfunctional play exists at all. Here, by "most existing theory," I primarily mean *developmental theories* of play.

> Contemporary theories of play . . . are concerned with the ways that play benefits children's psychological development. They have continued to impact on early childhood programs, particularly in under-fives settings, where we now see play located at the heart of the curriculum and used as a vehicle for nurturing children's development across its various domains.[1]

Implicit in all development theories of play[2] is the assumption that the natural history and evolution of play documents some necessary and beneficial component of play vital to species survival. That is, play is deemed valuable, and that value is then awarded according to the functional benefits play provides.

However, if play is beneficial, then what exactly is beneficial about play that is risky, dangerous, and destructive? These and many other common and negative outcomes of play are either ignored by developmental theories or discounted by those theories as deviant abnormalities—or, in other words, as "bad" play.[3]

Yet the subjective pleasures of bad play[4] seem as direct, immediate, and engaging as those of good play. It is, then, difficult to explain why evolution has assigned the same visceral response to risky, harmful, and antisocial play as to safe, beneficial, and pro-social play.

There are some speculative answers. For instance, perhaps the pleasures of bad play are a vestigial response and, in humans, bad play indeed no longer serves the same species functions as it did and does within lower animals. Or perhaps the function of bad play is more positive at the group level of analysis than at the individual level; in this case, bad play would, in effect, sacrifice the welfare of the individual for the welfare of the group. Or, perhaps, on balance, bad play is more advantageous than its more obvious risks and harms would superficially indicate.

There is, at present, no firm evidence supporting these speculations. And, regardless, the perception of risky and harmful play remains clearly negative within developmental theories of play—and elsewhere. Even when the pleasures of bad play are acknowledged in less than serious, non-theoretical contexts—in popular works of art and fiction, for instance—these pleasures are commonly attributed to animal, primitive, or otherwise irrational and, thus, undesirable origins. Yet these pleasures, guilty or not, remain.

And so, *why bad play?* In the remainder of this chapter, I am going to try to answer that question regarding two potentially inclusive categories of generic bad play: play that is threatening, risky, or otherwise *harmful* to the self or others; and play that is *against the rules.* Of these two, the former can be considered a *functional* definition of bad play; the latter can be considered, in contrast, a *formal* definition of bad play.

HARMFUL PLAY

Much play that is physically threatening or risky to players is also pleasurable and is, for that reason, actively sought by those players who put themselves most at risk. This category of risky but enjoyable play includes so-called extreme sports, as well as less competitive but equally dangerous behaviors: bungee jumping, skydiving, riding roller coasters, and the like. Indeed, the pleasures of these activities seem, to a great degree, determined by the amount of risk involved.

Putting someone other than yourself at risk during play includes bullying and other aggressive forms of childhood play—sometimes labeled "dark play."[5] In fact, aggressiveness toward others has long been cited as an indication of bad, inappropriate, and antisocial play[6] among children and adults. However, just as putting yourself at risk may be considered appropriate or inappropriate, pleasurable or not, depending on the context, putting others at risk may also be interpreted and valued differently in different contexts.

Many violent sports—boxing, for instance—assume some risk to the participants. More informal yet still willfully aggressive play, either during play fighting[7] or during those circumstances in which play fighting and real fighting are blurred—for instance, within the movie *Fight Club* (1999) (or, perhaps, within hockey games)—provide pleasures and gratifications largely indistinguishable from those provided by non-aggressive and non-risky play.

This is true of many quite risky non-competitive games as well—as evident in the history of and popular fascination with Russian roulette. Originally appearing only in fiction (in a story written by Georges Surdez in 1937 for *Collier's* magazine), Russian roulette has become as widely known as it is infrequently practiced or "played." Indeed, the classification of Russian roulette as a form of play (rather than suicide) seems critical to its popular conceptualization as intriguing behavior. The movie *Deer Hunter* (1978) effectively dramatizes the peculiar appeal of playful acts of personal destruction—in this case, Russian roulette—which are representational and yet, simultaneously and paradoxically, have physically harmful and, therein, clearly non-representational consequences.

Significantly, many other types of pleasurable human behavior—most pointedly, sexual behavior—can also involve acts of aggression, dominance, submission, and, on occasion, pain, up to and including bondage and torture.[8] Labeled abnormal and psychopathic—and, as such, conventionally discouraged—such extreme risk-taking (and risk-enjoying) behaviors nevertheless frequently appear within human virtual contexts, such as pornography. And these conceptual representations of bad play have demonstrable critical, popular, and commercial appeal, as with the writings of the Marquis de Sade, the stories of Anais Nin, Peter Schaffer's *Equus,* and even, to some degree, Mel Gibson films. In light of such acknowledged guilty pleasures—*schadenfreude*—it is unclear whether harmful or risky play can be rightfully characterized as "bad" without necessary reference to some preexisting normative context.[9]

Fortunately, perhaps, digital media and computer games provide a relatively safe and less-threatening context for play than a more rough-and-tumble natural environment. Bad play with computer games poses little to no physical risk to players—although risky and harmful computer game play can still involve severe emotional and psychological consequences.[10]

Nevertheless, within interactive digital media contexts, bad play is infrequently physically harmful and more frequently typical of a larger and more inclusive category of bad play: play that breaks the rules.

PLAY AGAINST THE RULES

Most often, bad play with computer games is characterized by play against the rules. These rules may include rules prohibiting risky or harmful play, so that these two categories of bad play—functional and formal, risky/harmful and rules-breaking—are not mutually exclusive. Indeed, if rules prohibiting harmful play are both conventional and widespread (most are), then the rules-breaking category of bad play subsumes the risky/harmful category of bad play. This is particularly the case when discussing play within virtual environments and—most pertinent to our discussion here—computer game play.

FORMS OF RULES

All computer games have some objective, explicit, and formal representations of their rules embedded in their software or *code.* For this reason, computer games provide a relatively straightforward context for distinguishing what is and what is not rules-appropriate play. This is true despite ongoing social negotiations regarding rules, which always seem part of playful social contexts, and despite the potential of emergent play resulting from either loosely constructed or poorly understood rules. Thus, to avoid any confusion over what the rules actually are, we can define rules-breaking play—and any so-called bad play associated with it—as play not explicitly allowed by the rules *as represented by the game code*.

Breaking some portion of a game's rules—for example, rules governing the mechanics of the game's interface—may make playing that game impossible. Also, players may—and, frequently do, particularly during initial computer game play—disconnect the game's power supply (i.e., pull the plug) or in some other way physically disturb, interrupt, or step beyond the game's coded rules context.[11]

While these can be considered examples of transgressive and, therein, rules-breaking play, the most interesting category of this type of play involves players who break the rules while engaging (rather than destroying) the game code. Given such a circumstance, rules-breaking play can be understood as playing *with* (rather than within or according to) the coded rules of the game. This play is then in conflict not only with the rules but also with the "spirit" of the game as interpreted by other players and, significantly, by the game designer(s). Such transgressions in computer game play are commonly called *exploits*.

This particular class of rules-breaking play—exploiting—involves breaking game rules while still maintaining some level of integrity within the rules system (or game *context*) of which the broken rules are a part. Thus, bad play of this sort is one of the more paradoxical and, therein, one of the more formally interesting manifestations of computer game play.

Despite the programmed and tangible nature of rules embedded in game code, computer game players seem to play as often in disregard of these rules as they do in accordance with them. To some extent, this behavior results when computer game designs (either intentionally or not) hide rules from players—as is frequently the case when computer games involve themes of exploration, mystery, or subterfuge. However, a great deal of rules-breaking play can also be observed among players who have full access to and full knowledge of game rules yet still willfully choose to ignore these rules in order to access a freer (and usually more effective) style of play.

Examples of exploitive play are extremely common within complex online role-playing games, for instance, which typically display a characteristically incomplete and continually revised rules set. Here, for instance, Maleki, a *World of Warcraft* (*WoW*) in-game support manager, explains the nature and consequences of a particular *WoW* exploit:

> To be a little more specific, the guild in question was using repeated line of sight exploits which prevented the mobs from attacking back. Also, using a pulling exploit which allowed them to only agro boss mobs. Both are considered exploits, and the guild in question was previously warned the night before. We want to reiterate that exploitation of high end content will not be tolerated.[12]

Exploits which use unintended rules conflicts or consequences to aid play are common in offline, single-player games as well—even including exploits provided by the game designers themselves in the form of so-called cheat codes. In fact, realizing the widespread tendency of players to explore, manipulate, and transform game rules to their advantage, many game designers have attempted to incorporate rules-breaking play within rules-appropriate play through special forms of rules: self-reflexive and self-transformative rules.

These "special" rules allow, in effect, game rules to be broken as an acceptable, appropriate, and sometimes necessary component of game play: they are rules to break rules. While the most obvious example of such a formal rules-breaking design is the cheat code, there are other, more subtle variations.

Within the several popular versions of Sid Meier's *Civilization* series of computer games, for instance, there is the self-transforming feature of World Wonders. When World Wonders—the Pyramids, Michelangelo's Chapel, and such—are introduced into the game, they transform the game rules, including those rules that allow subsequent World Wonders to be built. And, in fact, within most other, non-computer-based games—sports, poker, even solitaire—there are also frequent rules modifications, variations, and transgressions that serve to extend and enliven play within, ostensibly, those same boundaries established by the original game context.[13]

However, rules transformations in non-computer games are very often the result of social negotiations undertaken in normative contexts outside the game's rules system entirely.[14] The interactive nature of digital media makes it possible to include something like this negotiation process within the computer game design itself. That is, computer game designs provide a formal mechanism for recursively transformative—*rules-breaking*—processes.

During all initial computer game play, for instance, players make important game decisions prior to full knowledge of the game rules. Players must decide where to build founding cities in *Civilization* prior to full knowledge of the game's world map; similarly, players must decide what sort of characters to build within online role-playing games prior to full knowledge of the relative abilities and disabilities of character classes in MMOs.

In the former instance, the game rules of *Civilization* might be considered purposefully hiding information from players in order to introduce random elements of play. In the second instance, however, the game rules (i.e., MMO rules manuals) are simply incapable of describing character abilities that are only determined most definitely within a constantly shifting and largely player-determined context of play. This latter circumstance is not merely the result of social play. It is equally true of all popular action/arcade games in which contexts are determined entirely through individual play. In both contexts—social and solo—the *experience* of play is considered by players to be a better teacher (and evaluator) of game rules than any text-based explication or secondhand account.

In situations like these—where game rules must, in effect, bootstrap themselves during game play—players constantly make and remake in-game decisions based on what they (mostly mistakenly) *believe* are the game rules. These decisions then affect subsequent rules-determined game outcomes and forms. During this play and replay process, computer games are started and restarted, loaded and reloaded; game representations (e.g., *Civilization* starting positions, MMO avatars) are valued and revalued, rolled and re-rolled, built and rebuilt, constructed and destroyed—all without ever having full knowledge of the game rules, and all in order to conform, eventually and recursively, to those game rules as they are imbedded in the game code. Such repetitive and recursive play results in—and, simultaneously, is made necessary by—the characteristic incompleteness (either in perception or fact) of computer game rules.

Thus, whether the game rules and game design structures explicitly (in their code) allow such things to happen or not, the form of computer game play consistently displays *recursive contextualization*—through which rules are transformed during continuous, repeated, and, most important, recursive reference to those rules.

RULES AS SEMIOTIC FORMS

In order to discuss the implications of recursive contextualization during computer game play, let us consider computer game rules as *algorithms*.

These algorithms then also serve as *signs* (or references) pointing to some other object, process, or goal.

For example, game rules governing the movement of cars within *Grand Theft Auto* (*GTA*) point (or refer) to the movement of cars in three-dimensional city-spaces. It is then useful to think of these isolated car-moving algorithms in *GTA* as similar to the algorithms of more realistic simulations, such as *Microsoft's Flight Simulator* (*MFS*), which are quite explicit in establishing a real-world relationship between game form and game reference. However, the relationship of the game of *GTA* to real theft, crime, violence, and cars— or the relationship of the game of *SimCity* to real cities, or the relationship of the game of *Civilization* to real civilizations—is quite different from the relationship of the *simulation* of *MFS* to real airplanes. *GTA*'s "algorithms," as is the case with most computer games, are dedicated to providing an engaging and enjoyable game-playing experience. *MFS*'s algorithms, as is the case with most simulations, are dedicated to modeling a particular mechanic of physics: fixed-wing flight.

Is the *experience* of play, then, shaped by the same rules—that is, by the same algorithmic forms and functions—as are the *mechanics* of flight? No. This becomes clear when we realize rules-breaking (bad) play within computer *simulations* is different from rules-breaking play within computer *games*.

We most often characterize rules-breaking play within simulations, such as *MFS*, as unlearned, unpracticed, or unskilled play. That is, players who are ignorant of the rules of the simulation break those rules and play "badly." Over time, these players learn the rules of the simulation and how to play well by conforming to those rules. Thus, we might consider the initial "bad" play within simulations to be ultimately functional: that is, bad play serves as a necessary prelude to subsequently better and, eventually, "good" play.

In games, however, this same form of bad play never seems to get "better." Game players who have increasingly complete knowledge of game rules still use that knowledge to sustain and improve the "bad" play of rules breaking. So, although we might label the outcome of ignorant bad play to be rules learning (and thus functional) and the outcome of knowledgeable bad play to be rules breaking (and thus dysfunctional), there are no clear formal differences between the two.

Both rules-breaking processes—in simulations and in games—tend to conceptually transform rules and the play experience that those rules evoke. And both sorts of bad play—whether ignorant or knowing—serve to accomplish the same function: to discover and explore exactly what the rules *are*.

Thus, both during game play and during simulation use, the rules-breaking function of bad play closely parallels the function of so-called *Garfinkeling*:[15] breaking game rules is necessary to establish the presence and, relatedly, the contextual (or experiential) function of those game rules.

Significantly, then, in advanced computer game play—as opposed to advanced simulation use—rules-breaking play does not decrease. The process of rules discovery, exploration, and exploitation does not end. During "play" with simulations, the more practiced and expert player displays both more skill and, in demonstration of that skill, more rules-abiding behavior; the more practiced and expert player of computer games, on the other hand, also displays more skill, but, in demonstration of that skill, is increasingly likely to be rules intolerant. Thus, the use of simulations, in opposition to the play of games, does not display the same continuously recurring forms of recursive contextualization, either in original design or during prolonged play.

Indeed, a great percentage of *all* play with computer games can be classified as recursive contextualization, regardless of the knowledge or expertise (or lack thereof) of the game players. The only portion of computer game play that does not consistently display patterns of recursive contextualization—resulting in successive conceptual transformations of game rules—is that portion of play involving the manipulation of the computer game's physical interface: learning how to move the joystick or what keys to push on the keyboard.

For, within computer games, the algorithms governing the game interface point to something other than the subjective play experience: they point to the means to access that experience. Their function in this regard is then similar to the algorithms of a simulation. Once players have full knowledge of and sufficient practice with algorithms of the interface, these algorithms become increasingly habitualized and, therein, incapable of easy, useful, or enjoyable transformation. Indeed, subsequent transformations in game rules must take place within precisely such a learned and *fixed* context—or interface—which then provides a necessary, stable, and conceptually unassailable "ground"[16] for further assignation of relatively unstable values and meanings.

Learning the game interface is, therefore, more comparable to simulation use than to game play. For, once interface rules have been learned, play with those rules ends. Once the computer game interface has been mastered, computer play thereafter occurs not with (or against) but through (or within) the game interface; play is then increasingly focused on the manipulation of other, more subjective components of the play experience: the game code rather than the game hardware.

The subjective components of the game play experience are relational and combinatorial, and so it is rare that players exhaust all these possibilities during a single episode of play—or expect to. For this reason, game rules requiring a simple and linear, singular and focused manipulation of the game code—such as those manipulations guided by embedded narrative structures—quickly become intrusive and, eventually, during repeated play, superfluous to the game-playing experience.

Computer games played by longtime and expert players inevitably take on less of a "rigid-rule" and more of a "free-form"[17] structure, in which play is determined by, if any one thing in particular, the player's own localized and individualized sensation and experience. And it is at this stage that a conceptual transformation of rules— recursive contextualization—is most likely to transgress the original game context and engage the so-called metagame.

Within action/arcade games, for instance, this stage of play might include the creation of graphic contexts (e.g., wad files in *DOOM*) that then extend play within the context of the game's original interface; within MMOs, it might include more active participation and leadership in those social activities conducted outside the limited scope of the game's fantasy world; within strategy games, such as *Civilization,* it might include more abstract play with the game rules themselves; and so on. Or, alternatively, at this stage, the original game is simply placed aside, and a new game is taken up in its place.

During this culminate stage of expert and endgame play, it is interesting to note parallels with how game designers play their own games. During the design process, for instance, game designers have the unprecedented ability to play outside the rules of the game—and thus engage in rules-breaking ("bad") play. In this and many other respects,[18] play by game designers ignores the boundaries and restrictions placed on conventional game players.

Playing with rules in the manner of game designers is common within all free-form games and within all self-sustaining biological systems (e.g., ecosystems)—and certainly within the broader context of evolutionary biology. Yet attempting to implement free-form game play within coded game rules inevitably causes self-referential paradoxes: rules that break themselves. And if those paradoxes are not trapped and handled properly, the game defaults.

Suber (1990) and others[19] have noted the potentially self-destructive paradoxes that result when rules-based political, social, and biological systems attempt to transform those rules systems of which they are themselves part. Suber, in fact, has constructed a general case illustrating this problem of self-reflexive and self-transformative rules within the game *Nomic*. *Nomic*, a "game of self-amendment," is most fundamentally characterized by its rule 213.

213. If the rules are changed so that further play is impossible, or if the legality of a move cannot be determined with finality, or if by the Judge's best reasoning, not overruled, a move appears equally legal and illegal, then the first player unable to complete a turn is the winner. This rule takes precedence over every other rule determining the winner.[20]

Thus, *Nomic* is a simulation of a rules-making process, wherein winning conditions are determined by, in effect, breaking the rules of that process. In parallel, play itself may be understood—in the same Garfinkeling sense mentioned earlier—as a simulation of a *simulated* rules-making process. For just as *Nomic* simulates breaking the rules of a game, play simulates breaking the rules of simulating.

Here, however, it is vital that play remain a simulation (or an algorithmic *representation*) of a rules-breaking process, rather than that process itself, since if play were the latter, it would remain bound by the mechanics (i.e., the rules) of that process. However, as a *representation* of that process, play (or, more generally, *playing*) is free to transform rules of any sort—including rules related to the rules-breaking process—without having any permanent (and potentially disastrous) impact on the biological and cognitive restraints and forms that evoke and sustain play itself.

Similarly, *Nomic* must retain its position as a *game* of self-amendment, rather than the self-amendment process itself. Otherwise, *Nomic* might unravel itself. For while the self-amendment process that *Nomic*'s rules refer to remains paradoxical and, ultimately, untransformable, the *simulation* of that process within the game manages to amend rules in such a way that those amendments have no lasting effect on the broader and more inclusive process of self-amendment. Thus, *Nomic*, as a game, is unable to transform the play of self-amendment to which its rules refer. Or, more precisely, if it were to do so, then, according to rule 213, the game would immediately end.

This, then, is the crucial point at which the rules (algorithms) of simulations, games, and play diverge. While game rules may be unbound by the game context and thus capable of self-reflection, self-transformation, and, indeed, even self-destruction through their simultaneous and paradoxical application, the rules of play are irrevocably bound to and limited by their biological context. Thus, play cannot fail to produce paradox, and, somewhat paradoxically, play cannot fail to survive the paradoxes it produces.

For these reasons, it is useful to think of the algorithms and rules of games as occupying an intermediate position between the algorithms and rules of simulations and the algorithms and rules of play. The former are bound by context; the latter are not. The algorithms and rules of games are then "sort of" (and always temporarily) bound by context.

Since the algorithms and rules of games, simulations, and play are *representations,* we can position each as separate categories of *semiotic form* based on what they represent and how they represent it (e.g., either strictly or loosely). As figure 1.1 indicates, the algorithms and rules of simulations point to an objective process (i.e., "reality"), the algorithms and rules of games point to a subjective experience (i.e., "fun"), and the algorithms and rules of play point to the pointing (or representational) process itself. It is in this sense that play may be considered a simulation of *simulating.*

A game such as *Nomic* is, then, perhaps the closest possible "good" (non-rules-breaking) implementation of a play process that is, most fundamentally, "bad" (rules-breaking). Or, in other words, if you play with a simulation, it becomes a game; if you play with a game, it becomes just play; and if you play with play—well, you can't play with play: *play pwnz.*

Thus, rules-breaking of the sort that most characterizes bad play has a definite formal structure with an indefinite functional outcome. This formal structure provides for the evaluation, manipulation, and transformation of existing rules structures—forcibly so. And the outcome of this process is most typically paradox.

The representational and interactive qualities of computer games allow the construction of rules—like those in *Nomic*—that allow game players to engage in play analogous to that of game design. In a recursive contextualization process, computer game rules are then manipulated and transformed indefinitely *so long as those game rules remain incomplete.* However, should a rules system be finalized in some rigid (i.e., fully coded) form, then game play must thereafter either descend into the "good" and rules-abiding play of simulation use or ascend into the increasingly "bad" play of rules breaking. In the latter instance, play ultimately either breaks or abandons game rules.

Whether this formal, rules-breaking process of bad play is functional or dysfunctional, then, entirely depends on the quality (level of completeness) of the game rules and, simultaneously, on the social and cultural (or theoretical) context within which those rules are valued and given meaning.

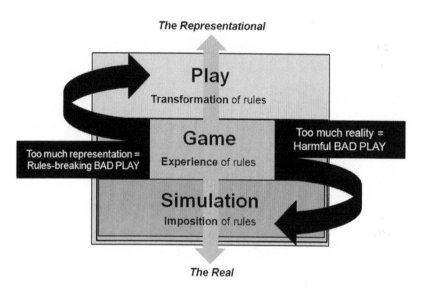

Semiotic Form	Formal Reference	Functional Outcome
Play Rules determined by **play**	Representation	Pretense
Game Rules determined by **player(s)**	Experience	Interaction
Simulation Rules determined by **designer**	Reality	Model

Figure 1.1. Relationships among play, games, and simulations

The Representational

Play
Transformation of rules

Game
Experience of rules

Too much representation =
Rules-breaking BAD PLAY

Too much reality =
Harmful BAD PLAY

Simulation
Imposition of rules

The Real

Figure 1.2. Representations of bad play

CONCLUSIONS

This chapter introduces a formal approach to the study of computer games and, in particular, to the study of a common component of computer game play often discounted by cultural analysis: bad play. While functional analyses of game play tend to distinguish between good and bad play based on their culturally relative consequences and associated values, a more formal analysis can demonstrate similarities between the two and, in fact, as has been suggested here, prioritizes the "bad" play as the more fundamental of the two. This sheds a new perspective on the nature and origin of the so-called good play that is most often supported and promoted by developmental theories: it may not be so "good" after all. Likewise, this perspective allows us to see "good" and "bad" players in a much different—and more equal—light.

Formal analysis also demonstrates how focusing on references and referencing—that is, on *semiosis*—can help us understand how human meaning-making processes function during the self-reflections and self-transformations of play. As those meaning-making processes are turned increasingly inward through recursive contextualization, the consequences of game play become not the meanings and values of the rules of the games but the paradoxes and devaluations of the forms of games.

Acknowledging a formal distinction between play and game implies that at least one function of game play must be to maintain that distinction—that is, to restrict and, where necessary, *punish* free and uninhibited play. Thus, we are motivated by this analysis to look for game structures that restrict and limit play—structures that are easily and widely found in all those (primarily developmental and educational) contexts that prioritize the algorithms and rules of simulations.

Can such restrictions be imposed successfully and fruitfully? Can the energies and pleasures of play as a whole be harnessed to accentuate the positive and de-emphasize the negative? Can bad play be tamed? As the following chapter will show, I think and hope not.

The success of any "serious"[21] or "persuasive" game (these were called "edutainment" in an older, pre-digital age) would necessarily depend on, in some important way, distorting and curtailing the natural progression of human play as a rules-breaking process. This may be tantamount to trying to teach human beings either a new way to see while using the same old retina or a new way to speak while using the same old larynx. It's possible, perhaps, but tedious and awkward compared to the original. Trying to teach human beings a new way to play using the same old cognition requires less promoting the new than suppressing the old. And human play may well be (again, hope seems in order) irrepressible.

If so, then an irrepressible play appears to have a dual function within all game-like rules structures: it delimits and explicates those structures, and, simultaneously, it creates paradoxical contexts within which those rules structures are either transformed or broken (or both).

These two related functions are, in brief, profound. They are as necessary for the existence of games as they are predictive of the fragile and impermanent nature of games. And, importantly, theories of play that have no primary explanatory role for common and widespread "bad" play should be questioned solely on that basis. Of available theories of play, *agonistic* theories[22] best offer an interpretation of play consonant with the position presented here, yet those theories also commonly seek refuge in normative contexts in order to distinguish the good from the bad.

An important theoretical advantage offered by a formalist approach is that, without recourse to normative contexts, it is possible to justify the existence of bad play as a necessary and unavoidable consequence of the peculiar and related representational forms of simulations, games, and play.

CHAPTER 2

Anti-ness

> Did He smile His work to see?
> Did He who made the lamb make thee?
>
> —William Blake, *Songs of Experience* (1794)

PLAY WITH FORM

Games are designed to be played, just as books are designed to be read. Both playing a game and reading a book involve transforming a predetermined set of rules into a more immediate phenomenological experience. And, of course, reading includes a larger set of behaviors than just reading books, just as playing includes a larger set of behaviors than just playing games.

However, there are important differences between the two. Reading, for instance, is a learned behavior and, therein, an unnatural behavior—particularly in comparison to play. Literacy is a difficult goal to achieve and, for that reason, remains unachieved by large segments of the human population. Play, on the other hand, is widespread, more analogous to some difficult-to-eradicate weed than to the cultivated rose of reading. Play can be motivated and directed by game rules but also appears without evocation by game design; for this reason, the "rules" of play seem, at least in some significant part, preformed and hardwired within human beings.

And, curiously, reading a book—and other forms of related aesthetic experiences, such as viewing a film—demand some measure of solitude and passivity; play, on the other hand, demands some measure of precisely the opposite. While play can certainly be quiet and contemplative, we prototypically describe human play using physically determinable categories similar to those used to describe animal play:[1] locomotor play (e.g., leaping, soaring, brachiating—or, in general, play with *body*), object play (including play with *conceptual* objects within computer games), and social play (play with *others*).

Each of these categories is an active form of *playing with* something, and it will be my contention here that this characteristic form of *playing with* is fundamental to human play and, further, that this form is similar regardless of who or what is being played with.

If human play conforms to the three categories of play just mentioned, then objects and forms of play can also be one of three sorts: objects and forms involving the manipulation of the interface between our bodies and our environment (during locomotor play), objects and forms involving the transformation of physical sensations into conceptual objects (the same process as that of semiosis), and objects and forms involving the construction, maintenance, and sustenance of relationships with others (during social play).

A FORMALIST ASIDE

When I refer to "objects" of play, I mean to refer to real-world objects, such as dogs and trees, footballs and joysticks, but also, more important, to the values of these objects as those values are determined by representational form. Necessarily intertwined with real-world objects and their in-game representations is then another vital component: the relationship between the two. While objects and their representations may vary widely, the relationship between objects and their representations has a particular and constant set of forms, which I wish to emphasize here.

For instance, most are familiar with the game of tic-tac-toe (TTT). Normally, TTT can be recognized by its well-known crosshatch playing field and its conventional playing pieces: Xs and Os. Yet neither of these two game objects—field or pieces—is critical to the formalist. The most fundamental property of any game, according to the formalist, involves the relationships among game objects that determine the values of those objects within the game.

In part, these relationships are described by the rules of the game, which prioritize and therein value game objects during play; but the rules of the game may be expressed in different languages and in different ways. So, again, the surface appearance of the rules—whether these rules are written in, for instance, French or English—is immaterial. It is the relationships these rules refer to, not the rules themselves, that constitute the form of the game.

Imagine, for instance, another game (let's call it T3) consisting of nine tiles, labeled a1, a2, a3, b1, b2, b3, c1, c2, and c3. In the game of T3, two players alternate picking tiles, each attempting to select tiles that will create an a-b-c sequence, a 1-2-3 sequence, or both. Further imagine a set of rules for T3 that would eliminate from selection any sequences in T3 (e.g., "a1-c2-b3" or "a3-b1-c1") that would not conform to the winning conditions of TTT. At this point, the game of T3, without a crosshatch playing field and without any Xs or Os, is formally identical to TTT. We might, at this point, say that the rules of TTT are more easily understood or, perhaps, more "elegant" than the rules of T3, but both sets of rules point or refer to the same essential form. For the formalist, the elements of TTT and T3 that are dissimilar are inconsequential, and the elements of TTT and T3 that are similar are fundamental.

One technique of the formalist, then, is to identify and distinguish forms and relationships referenced by game rules and, in that process, to try to find the most efficient or "elegant" way of describing those forms and relationships. However, while game play is guided by game rules, it is not, in all cases, determined by game rules. Game rules can themselves become objects of play, and formal relationships among objects of play within games can be extended to include formal relationships between games and players and, indeed, between games and play itself. As a consequence, the importance of isolated objects and their values within games is diminished, and the importance of relationships among objects and their values as these are realized *during play* is increased.

This realization would require the computer game formalist to be something of a phenomenologist as well—to seek the fundamental form of object-value relationships (if such a form exists) that coincides most closely with the immediate and subjective experience of play.

ANTI-FORM

A characteristic form of human play, regardless of the objects being played with, embodies a reference to what is not—or to something other than what is. It is useful to think of this as a "not" or "anti-"form. That is, when we ride a stick horse, it is not a horse, it is something else—something like a horse, but not a horse: it is an anti-horse, which requires but does not fulfill its reference to a horse. Likewise, during play we might pretend that a box is a house, that stacked wooden cylinders are a king, or a that finger is a gun.

This anti-form can then be applied, self-referentially, to play itself. Bateson[2] identified this particular form and its peculiar consequences as the single most fundamental characteristic of play in animals and in humans: play as meta-communication. That is, all forms of play transmit a self-referential message: "this is play" or, alternatively, "this is not real."

When we play with objects, for instance, those objects are not what they are; when we play with others, those others are, for the moment, not others. And when we play with self, that self is something other than what it is: an *anti*-self.

The so-called magic circle[3] of play attempts to distinguish between what lies on either side of this anti-form: the real and the make-believe, the necessary and the frivolous. However, the contents of play—those objects and forms that are played with—are, again, less characteristic of the play experience than are the formal properties of the boundary condition itself. This boundary condition results from negation, or not-ness, or from what I will call here an *anti*-form.

As a formalist (and a biological naturalist), I begin with play as an embodied mechanism—an anti-form—that acts upon (plays with) objects and their values (i.e., their contextual representations) within an organism's natural environment. During this process, these objects and values are transformed, with a variety of consequences, but, assumedly, according to a single and common formal mechanism.

This common mechanic of anti-form is most evident as a self-referential function operating on representations of objects: *re*-presenting representations. In fact, the evolution of a human-like cognition may be closely associated with—and depend on—such self-reference. The self-references of an anti-form are then simultaneously similar to themselves and different from themselves, with their most important consequences being predictability and variability.

This ability to provide useful variation through repetition is neatly encapsulated by Sutton-Smith in his notion of "adaptive variability" as a primary function of human play.

> In looking for what is common to child and adult forms of play, to animal and human forms, to dreams, daydreams, play, games, sports, and festivals, it is not hard to reach the conclusion that what they have in common, even cross culturally, is their amazing diversity and variability. The possibility then arises, that it is this variability that is central to the function of play throughout all species.[4]

The analysis I present here is sympathetic to this definition, sharing with it the belief that play is understood best within a naturally evolved biological system.

However, Sutton-Smith positions his definition as inclusive of alternative points of view, particularly those culturally oriented (e.g., developmental) theories in which human play is subsumed within theories of learning and, even more restrictively, within theories of education. Theories emphasizing the role of play in a particular cultural context tend to distinguish some portion of human play from animal play in order to position human play as an intellectual achievement rather than as a vestigial mechanic. I will focus more narrowly on those forms of play that are assumed to have neither allegiance nor debt to cultural values and social norms.

Here, I consider play a self-reflexive, formal process that operates most significantly *on its own form*. If so, then cultural content is largely irrelevant to the operation and consequences of that anti-form.

Similarly, an aesthetic of play is a self-reflexive aesthetic that operates most significantly on its own form: the human aesthetic process. Since this peculiar aesthetic of play is self-reflexive, self-transformative, and, ultimately, self-destructive, I will label this aesthetic of play an *anti*-aesthetic.

ANTI-AESTHETICS

An aesthetics of the anti-aesthetics does not imply a negation of aesthetics. Rather, it is intended to refer to negation itself and an accompanying aesthetics of negation; or, alternatively, to an aesthetics of opposition; or, alternatively, to an aesthetics of the *anti*. Bolter and Grusin (2000) have popularized the notion of *re*-mediation as fundamental to the function of digital media, and here the emphasis is similar. I wish to consider the origin, nature, and pleasures of digital game *re*-presentations and the resulting *anti*-ness of digital game forms.

Of all those characteristics distinguishing the aesthetic experience of digital media—and, particularly, the experience of computer game play— the repetitiveness of that experience is most obvious. In other, older and (more conventionally) less-interactive media, aesthetic pleasures appear more quickly and more directly. For instance, the enjoyment of the visual, aural, and kinesthetic arts[5] is as much in the moment of sensation as in either delayed reflection or persistent repetition. Admittedly, of course, to some extent, this is also true of computer games—particularly as regards certain genres (e.g., first-person shooters, perhaps)—which employ visual signs appealing directly to the senses and thus invoking a mechanical and, often, involuntary response.

However, regardless of the quality of images employed, the digital interface of computer games allows no direct and immediate access to its patterns and designs. Digital game images are always images in motion, and that motion is always in reference to something else: the game code. The necessities of the digital game interface delay and, subsequently, contextualize aesthetic experience within the rules of the game or, eventually and inevitably, within interactive and self-reflexive play.

Thus, in contrast to other, non-digital aesthetic forms, through continuous repetition and recursion, computer games access and return to a single and particular moment of formal engagement, which is, during that return, habitualized, contextualized, and re-engaged as a novelty of false experience: anti-experience. This peculiar aesthetic experience is, then, both like and unlike the experience of more traditional aesthetic forms.

Poetic language, for instance, may well repeat its own formal properties—rhyme, verse, stanza—but these properties are not most fundamentally characterized by the discontinuities of subsequent semiotic transformations. Though much of art and art forms—particularly literary forms—possess some portion of the recursive and self-reflexive characteristics of digital media, the latter posses those characteristics most obviously, most strongly, and most pointedly during computer game play.

I will therefore argue here that the root of an extended, repetitive, and formal engagement with the rules and mechanics of aesthetic form, as displayed during computer game play, is the result of a deeply rooted anti principle accentuated by the malleable and discontinuous nature of digital media. And, further, I would claim that this principle originates within a natural and largely intractable human semiosis. To this end, before we move onward, let me briefly introduce a few antecedents to this anti-ness.

ANTI-PHILOSOPHY

Doubt occupies a central position in many of the more perplexing problems of human epistemology. Descartes' famous aphorism "Cogito, ergo sum" is less persuasive than it is tautological until replaced by the more reasonable "Dubito, ergo sum." For, among all cognitive functions, doubt is the single function incapable of being doubted and, thus, the single function that carries the artifice of human thought, like a turtle, on its back.

If you would be a real seeker after truth, it is necessary that at least once in your life you doubt, as far as possible, all things.[6]

Hegelian dialectics emphasizes the critical role of antithesis as a catalyst for subsequent synthesis and historical progression. Later philosophical inquiry disassociates antithetical forms from a Hegelian, suprarational context and examines the implications of those forms within the tangled hierarchies of more socially relevant domains. Within phenomenological and existentialist philosophy, for instance, doubt, denial, and resulting conflicts between self and other are associated with personal freedom and independence of will.

A core anti principle might then be found at the base of human despair (Kierkegaard) and as the cause of human enlightenment (Nietzsche). And a similar principle might be located in the radical skepticism of postmodern aesthetics, marked by the nihilist leanings of dadaism, punk rock, and all those other deconstructions of the popular.

Indeed, the seeming lack of any embedded order or coherence in the vast data constructs of digital media (e.g., the World Wide Web) is accompanied by our persistent human desire to drill, Google-like, down to some single datum of individual self-interest. This desire well represents the inclination of the anti to identify and prioritize the singular, the distinctive, and the selfish.

Spencer-Brown (1972) positioned the fundamental function of all logic (and, in fact, of all cognition) as exactly this: a generic and primitive mark of distinction that must precede any subsequent separation of self and other.

Merrill (1995) helps clarify the pervasiveness of this distinction:

At this more primitive level, all acts of distinction and indication are identical; qualitative differences are smoothed out, and focus is reduced to the mere act of creating boundaries separating this from that. All distinctions, indications, and values are thus treated alike.[7]

However, while such a broadly conceived anti principle is clearly associated with the negation or the opposition of some other, this principle is not as often or as willingly associated with a bland and blanket nihilism.

Among other things I wished to translate and adapt to my own ends the Heideggerian word *Destruktion* or *Abbau*. Each signified in this context an operation bearing on the structure or traditional architecture of the fundamental concepts of ontology or of Western metaphysics. But in French "destruction" too obviously implied an annihilation or a negative reduction much closer perhaps to Nietzschean "demolition" than to the Heideggerian interpretation or to the type of reading that I proposed.[8]

Thus, the anti principle I would conjure here is willful, primitive, self-serving, and universal in form. It may function destructively or constructively (or, in linguistic terms, with compositionality) in social domains. More readily distinguished by its generic form than its localized function, the anti is always indicative of human agency. And, therein, the dark and the negative and the antithesis are not simple intermediaries existing prior to some yet-to-evolve, more rational context; rather, the anti principle both drives and defines human rationality and all subsequent representational processes (most specifically semiosis) through which we access, measure, interpret, and value human experience.

Further, as a recursive function, this anti principle is self-similar and must exist both outside and in opposition to the boundaries of its own determination. That is, the anti function may operate without any formal argument other than itself.[9]

These two basic characteristics—self-similarity and formal independence—make the anti principle paradoxical and, for good or ill, incapable of conventional normative evaluation—or linguistic expression. Indeed, when looked at from within some normative context (i.e., from within the confines of some preexisting structure yet to be ravaged), the anti appears little more than simply dysfunctional—random, chaotic, incorrigible, and incomprehensible. Yet so does play appear—most particularly bad play, which we can now label anti-play.

ANTI-PLAY

The anti principle is well conceptualized as a form of human play. There is, in fact, some relevance and support for this association. Huizinga (1955) assigns a great deal of importance to opposition, conflict, and the concept of the agon in the continuously contested nature of play and games. This theme of agonistic play is then extended by Turner (1990) and, later, Spariosu (1997), who find diaspora and the "ludic-liminal" exile of self necessarily set apart from the logocentric rules and regulations of more rational and rationalized games.

I sometimes talk about the liminal phase being dominantly in the "subjunctive mood" of culture, the mood of maybe, might-be, as-if, hypothesis, fantasy, conjecture, desire, depending on which of the trinity, cognition, affect, and conation (thought, feeling, or intention) is situationally dominant . . . Liminality can perhaps be described as a fructile chaos. A fertile nothingness, a storehouse of possibilities, not by any means a random assemblage but a striving after new forms and structure, a gestation process, a fetation of modes appropriate to anticipating postliminal existence.[10]

Liminality is more than a passive, negative condition or the intermediary-mediating phase between two positive conditions . . . Liminality contains both positive and active qualities.[11]

The liminal is a particularly resonant anti-concept within play theory and the so-called magic circle. Conventional accounts of a magic circle (see Salen & Zimmerman 2003) emphasize the distinction between play and non-play. However, perhaps better in keeping with the original context of the term (see Copier 2005), the boundary condition itself—that is, the circling or separating function (cf. Nieuwdorp 2005)—is more fundamental and telling than any content encircled.

It is precisely play as a purely formal activity—serving only to distinguish itself from some other—that Caillois (1961) described as "pure waste." Very early play theory (Groos in *The Play of Man* in 1901) likewise found little reason to account advantageously for the random, chaotic, and destructive functions of play as a form of anti-work. And current play theory devoted to explaining the educational benefits of play (Gee 2003; Papert 1993) likewise does little to explain, justify, or even acknowledge the purely formal and/or actively negative consequences of an anti-play (e.g., anti-educational play) of animals and humans.

Most theories of play, in fact, neatly divide between, on one hand, the rational and the developmental theories concerned with the normative functions and benefits of so-called good play and, on the other hand, accounts of a more irrational and agonistic bad (or anti-) play involving Bacchanalian, Dionysian, and other seemingly irrational behaviors. It is only this latter group of theories that is likely to consider play as a formal mechanism (Caillois' *paideia*) that functions, if at all, to question, doubt, and/or deconstruct the rules of conventional society.

Perhaps because it remains so difficult to reconcile the wanton nature of play with its supposed educational and adaptive benefits, recent summaries of play theory (Salen & Zimmerman 2003; Raessens & Goldstein 2005) tend more often to compromise than to distinguish these separate conceptualizations. My goal here is to attribute all functions of play—positive and negative—to a single set of formal properties. Or, in short, an anti-aesthetic, like an anti-play, is selfish: it is and is only about itself.

CHAPTER 3

Formalism Redux

> Rationalism is a hideous monster
> when it claims for itself omnipotence.
> —Mahatma Gandhi, *Young India* (1926)

[OLD] MEDIA AESTHETICS

The use of formalist techniques in the humanities is rare these days, almost passé. Formalism has been largely absorbed and, indeed, almost eliminated by variants of structuralism, which have proven more appealing to those who would situate the study of everything—and most particularly the study of aesthetics—within the study of society.

A rigid formalism assumes that there are certain formal characteristics of objects—most particularly aesthetic objects—that determine their identity and their consequence, or their essence. Much of geometry and topology, for instance, are formalist fields of study. The "essence" of a square is determined by a formal relationship among its sides and angles; and, likewise, the topological definition of a torus is determined by a set of formal relationships that call our attention to what characteristics are common among all tori and what characteristics are superficial and thus inconsequential to the torus form.

One of the clearest and most influential statements of formalism in the arts—specifically, in literary analysis—came from a rather eclectic group of artists, writers, and critics living and working in eastern Europe during the early twentieth century. This group—later known in aggregate as Russian formalists—was reacting in part against the nineteenth-century practice of evaluating works of literature as products of a particular writer working in a particular venue. In order to understand the works of Shakespeare, for instance, according to this tradition, it was necessary to understand Shakespeare the man, as he lived and loved (or not) within sixteenth-century England.

In opposition to biographical analysis, the Russian formalists believed that the work of art itself was the only object necessary to understand and evaluate that work. In order to demonstrate this, these critics went to great lengths to isolate the formal essence of literature: its "literariness." It was then assumed that this essence of literary form—and this form alone, apart from either author intent or reader affect—defined and determined literature and set it apart from more mundane, practical, and everyday prose.

Slightly after the Russian formalist movement—well described in Erlich's *Russian Formalism*[1]—came a similar wave of publications from the so-called New Critics, a cadre of (primarily) poetry critics working in U.S. academia during the 1920s.

Wellek[2] assigns Viktor Shklovsky (*On the Theory of Prose,* 1925), Boris Eikhenbaum (*Melody of the Russian Lyrical Verse,* 1921), Yuri Tynyanov (*Archaists and Innovators,* 1925), and Boris Tomashevsky (*Russian Versification: Metrics,* 1923) leadership in the Russian formalist movement. In particular, Shklovsky's early essays make the explicit claim that "the literary work is nothing but form" and that all art is, in fact, "outside emotion." While Shklovsky's views may have been extreme among his fellows, the desire to isolate and analyze literature as a formal derivative of natural language was characteristic of the formalist approach on both continents.

Prominent within the American formalist movement were John Crow Ransom (*The New Criticism,* 1941), Cleanth Brooks (*The Well Wrought Urn,* 1947), and the aforementioned William K. Wimsatt, the originator (along with Monroe Beardsley) of the "affective" and "intentional" fallacies (*The Verbal Icon,* 1954). Like their Russian predecessors, American formalists eschewed literary analysis based on either intent of author (the intentional fallacy) or individual and private effects on readers (the affective fallacy). And, despite great differences in cultural backgrounds and political ideologies between the Russians and the Americans, these two early twentieth-century groups have come to be linked in their common goal of studying scientifically, measuring empirically, and defining objectively the formal properties of "literariness" (*literaturnost*).

FORMALIST TECHNIQUES

America's New Critics introduced the methodology now most closely associated with formalism and still the single most sustaining contribution of formalism to contemporary literary analysis: the "close reading" of texts. Close reading consciously avoids all interpretations referring to and depending on elements extrinsic to the text. During a close reading, formalist critics attempt to isolate objective components of texts—for example, rhythm, meter, and imagery in poetry—that are most characteristic of and fundamental to literary form.

As practiced by the New Critics, this close analytical technique is very similar to earlier, linguistics-inspired analyses conducted by the Russian formalists. Each is an attempt to introduce scientific methods to the study of literature and, by extension, the study of culture. And, while each was successful in identifying and cataloging meaningful components of human language,[3] each also suffered in its inability to move from an analysis of specific components of texts to an explication of more general principles of literature.

In its most isolated and restricted use, engaged solely in the effort to locate literariness, formalist methodology raises uneasy questions concerning the relative importance of literary *form* and literary *content*—or, later, concerning the relative importance of *structure* and *materials*. Further, close reading begs the question of how much knowledge of social context and use of language is required prior to objective formal analysis. And, indeed, the implicit requirement that the formalist critics possess some relatively advanced expertise prior to the application of formalist methods undermines the objectivity of those methods. It is for this reason that New Criticism, in particular, is often regarded—and criticized—as an elitist approach.

Alternative methods that acknowledge and include the influence of social context during literary analysis are of two basic sorts. The first sort—critical methods—applies non-formalist methodologies to an analysis of social and literary contexts. These methods subsume the professed objectivity of formalism within broader social conflict paradigms and, subsequently, within increasingly less formal and more *structural* models of art and society.

The second sort retains the objective premise of formalist techniques and applies those techniques both to individual components of texts and to the social contexts that produce them. These social contexts are then taken as indicative of contextual *systems*. Erlich, for instance, makes much of the methodological evolution of formal analysis to systems analysis, which then served as a precursor to the development of contemporary *semiotics*.

During the "heroic" period of Russian formalism, the science of signs was virtually non-existent . . . But by 1930, . . . this new discipline was well under way. The theory of language was being fitted into the larger framework of a philosophy of symbolic forms which considered language as the central, but not the only possible system of symbols.[4]

FORMALIST ASSUMPTIONS

> Poetry is language in its aesthetic function.
>
> —Roman Jakobson, *Noveishaya Russkaya Poeziya* (1921)

Russian formalism originated in ideological opposition to existing theories of literature (e.g., symbolism and impressionism), and the methods employed by formalists purposefully ignored preexisting theoretical contexts. However, formalism involves a linked set of assumptions about the nature of language and literature, which were neither often nor completely acknowledged by early formalists.

At the core of both Russian and American formalism is the notion that literature serves a particular aesthetic function apart from that of everyday, conventional language. In *Art as Technique*, Shklovsky describes the purpose of art as re-establishing the "process of perception." In this process, art "defamiliarizes" those objects to which it refers, creating a sense of strangeness called *ostranenie*. *Ostranenie* then *re*-engages the process of perception as that process exists prior to its mediation by language. During this re-engagement, literature functions in a manner somewhat akin to phenomenological "bracketing"; that is, literature defamiliarizes conventional language through a self-referential process.

This process entails a number of assumptions about the nature of language and mind. However, before preceding further, it is necessary to deal with the potentially misleading term *perception*—a term that Shklovsky purposefully disassociated from Aleksander Potebnia's earlier claim that art was "thinking in images."[5] Shklovsky and other formalists clearly repudiated this particular distinction between practical and poetic language; therefore, the "process of perception" referred to by formalists is perhaps better thought of, in a more general sense, as a process of *semiosis*—or, even more generally, as a process of *cognition*.

Given this interpretation, formalism can be recognized as an early form of cognitive science, with its goal being to find formal properties of sign and symbol systems indicative of formal properties of the mind.[6] And the most basic theoretical assumptions of formalism remain consonant with those of cognitive science—with one important omission. Those most basic assumptions are these:

- The function of literature is to evoke a subjective but universal human feeling (*ostranenie*), based on the common and consistent phenomenological properties of language—a common and consistent *aesthetic*. This feeling can be referenced objectively, though indirectly, within the sign and symbol system that evokes it.

- While formally and functionally distinct, poetic language and literature are part of the same sign and symbol system as conventional language. Literature uses the sign and symbol system of conventional language in unconventional ways—for example, in the form of trope or verse. Therefore, the literary function of language is not unique but *derivative* of the common function of language. Differences among characteristic types of language (poetic vs. non-poetic) are then differences based on sequence, syntax, or other objectively measured *forms*.

- The primary function of conventional language is to familiarize; the function of literary language (e.g., poetry), on the other hand, is to defamiliarize. Thus, the latter is dependent on and cannot occur without *reference* to the former—again emphasizing the derivative nature of literary form.

These three assumptions—that literature has universal form and effect, that literature is derivative of common forms of natural language, and that literature functions as a referential (or *self*-referential) form—justify the use of formalist theory and methods within the study of sign and symbol systems. However, it remains a bit of a stretch to position early formalism as a precursor to cognitive science without the further assumption that the subjective experience of literature originates within and is determined by *biological properties of the human brain*. This important assumption—of a *cognitive* aesthetic—was not a well-articulated part of the early formalist agenda. Currently, explanations of natural-historical origins and causes of human aesthetic experiences continue to remain outside formalist theoretical domains; and it is exactly this omission that has helped lead to the formalist demise.

Perhaps formalism succumbed to successive waves of structuralism (and, subsequently, post-structuralism) simply because cognitive science was too young then—and is too young now—to catalog properly the mechanics of the senses that guide and influence human aesthetics. For, if formalist models had been grounded, from the beginning, in a more sophisticated knowledge of human behavior and its biological precedents (e.g., in a sort of *biogenetic* structuralism),[7] then formalism might have been made more resistant to competing structural models.[8] Regardless of those possibilities, however, significantly missing from early formalist theory is a detailed explanation of just how—and for what reasons—*familiarization* takes place. Thus, even when stated in its most positivist guise, formalism remains reactionary and more clearly delineated by its methodology and critique of preexisting bodies of literary theory than by its own unique theoretical stance.

[NEW] MEDIA AESTHETICS

The argument I am offering here is, in parallel to that of early formalism, a rather simple one: digital games and interactive play occupy the same position relative to natural human semiosis that, for the Russian formalists, literature and poetic language occupy relative to conventional human language. Thus, the cognitive requirements for computer game play are parallel, in part, with requirements for reading. The initial process of learning computer game controls is analogous to the process of learning an alphabet, grammar, and syntax. In both cases, aesthetic pleasures are delayed during a period in which player/reader frustration is more likely than player/reader enjoyment.

This analogy is not strict, however. Once literacy has been mastered, there is no recurring requirement of the reader to further understand and access natural and conventional language. In computer game play, however, there are always new controls—and new rules—to learn. For this reason, the experience of computer game play is more properly compared to the experience of reading poetic language.

The demands of poetic language are more involved than those of conventional language. The experience of reading poetic language is, like the experience of playing a computer game, uncertain; a successful and pleasurable experience must include some measure of interactivity involving both the knowledge of and the ability to re-evaluate preexisting linguistic forms (e.g., the ability to recognize the capitalization, spelling, and punctuation "mistakes" of poet e. e. cummings).

Poetic language is therein a counterpoint to existing and conventional language—or, in the terms I used earlier, a sort of *anti*-language. Correspondingly, the function of poetic language is a direct result of its antiform: it is an undermining and questioning of existing linguistic models and a resulting confusion (or, on occasion, enlightenment) regarding those referents to which conventional language refers.

As Russian formalist Shklovsky famously observed, poetic language serves "to recover the sense of life, in order to feel objects, to make the stone stony."[9] Formalist claims that poetic language returns us to a pre-linguistic state are based on the function of conventional language as artifice: a virtual

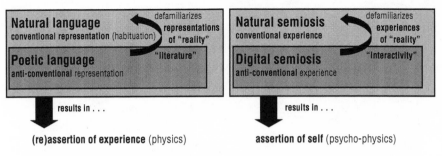

Figure 3.1. Formal parallels between language and semiosis

representation of real-world objects and sensations. In this function, conventional language distorts our real-world sensations; poetic language, in rebuttal, self-referentially calls our attention to the nature and origin of those distortions. Thus, poetic language is—and is not—part of the language system that contains it.

It is then useful to think of the function of literary form—and digital game form—as founded on an anti (or agonistic play) principle that repeats, recants, and therein reveals the otherwise hidden properties and mechanisms of the larger contexts to which they belong. If poetic language is a sort of anti-language, then digital games are a sort of anti-experience.

The ubiquitous controller of the computer game both is and is not a part of the human nervous system—the human experience—that contains it. By confining the experience of computer game play within the mechanics of the computer game controller and habituated response, computer game rules and relationships undermine and deny conventional experience in much the same manner that poetic language undermines and denies conventional language.

The great difference, however, is that poetic language merely points to— and is therein distinguished from—the human physical form. Regardless of the skill of the poet, poetic language is never so stony as the stone; rather, it *remakes* the stone stony. There is no similar and incontrovertible distinction made between the human physical form and the computer game, particularly under those circumstances where both systems—the human nervous system and the computer game platform/engine/interface—perform their functions subliminally. The computer game *makes* (rather than remakes) the computer game experience and therein confirms what poetic language would deny: the reality of the artifice.

During computer game play, the human body and the human experience are accessible only as these are represented and valued by computer game mechanics. Poetic language points us to an objective correlative: a pre-linguistic state of direct and immediate experience. Computer games, in contrast, point us to the psychophysical: what we believe to be true.

In parallel with the statement of Jakobson quoted earlier, we might then say that digital media play—and, most particularly, computer game play—is semiosis in its anti-aesthetic function.

THE FORMALIST PRECIPICE

Digital media provide rich opportunities for formal analysis, due to their reliance on an explicit and embedded *code*. In fact, most available formal analyses of media engage the relationship between media codes and human codes (e.g., language). There are several flavors of "media as code" theory, distinguished by the degree to which formal properties of digital code are assigned influence and priority over formal properties of human perception, cognition, and experience.

One of the more recent examples of a purely formalist approach, unfettered by contextual concerns, is Andersen's semiotic analysis of programming languages, in which he considers aspects of digital signs "unique to the computer medium.[10] This analysis de-emphasizes all affective and interpretive components of digital media, in favor of classifying digital code solely on the basis of its relationship to other sign and symbol systems. For instance, Andersen assigns a single set of objective properties to an "interactive" digital sign: an interactive sign accepts input, has mutable features, and can affect features of other signs. When using such a definition, no assumptions need be made concerning the function of interactive signs within human interpretive systems.

Others more strongly emphasize the importance of human interpretive systems and functions in interpreting digital code—and, correspondingly, give as much attention to aesthetic experiences as formal properties. Manovich, for instance, distinguishes between "transparent" and "non-transparent" digital code—terms that reference the ability of digital code to transform human thought.

> In cultural communication, a code is rarely simply a neutral transport mechanism; usually it affects the messages transmitted with its help. For instance, it may make some messages easy to conceive and render others unthinkable. A code may also provide its own model of the world, its own logical system,

or ideology; subsequent cultural messages or whole languages created using this code will be limited by this model, system, or ideology. Most modern cultural theories rely on these notions, which together I will refer to the "non-transparency of the code" idea.[11]

Formalist models would agree, in some sense, that digital media code is "non-transparent." However, formalist models diverge from those of cultural studies in the former's claim that digital media codes and forms—including, in significant part, the rules of computer game play—are governed by biological codes that are non-transmutable. That is, codes of technology and, ultimately, codes of culture come to resemble the interior mechanics—the biological "code"—governing construction of human experience.

If code is arbitrarily non-transparent—a position that some versions of cultural studies (and media determinism) take to the extreme—then formalism cannot remain "pure." Formalism remains valid only as the initial step in establishing a relationship between aesthetics and cognition, or, more strongly put, between codes of media and codes of brains. And, in fact, there is an even stronger cognitive-based position: the non-transparency of media code is itself an indication of its (non-arbitrary) origin. That is, the "ideology" of media code is non-transparent—and intractable—precisely because it parallels equally non-transparent, intractable (and yet mysterious) codes of biology.

It is now widely maintained that the concept of "literariness" has been critically examined and found deficient. Prominent postmodern literary theorists have argued that there are no special characteristics that distinguish literature from other texts. Similarly, cognitive psychology has often subsumed literary understanding within a general theory of discourse processing. However, a review of empirical studies of literary readers reveals traces of literariness that appear irreducible to either of these explanatory frameworks.[12]

The most important contribution of Russian formalism was its discovery of universal patterns within literary forms; yet, simultaneously, the great failure of formalism was its inability to reveal the origins of those patterns and forms. For this reason, Russian formalism quickly fell to the more explicit claims of Marxism, which was quicker and more certain in attributing aesthetic patterns and structures—indeed, the patterns and structures of all things—to a dialectical materialism shaping art and community. The influence of classical Marxism has since diminished but has been replaced by structural variants that have continued to suppress the occasional formalist revival, wherein each structural and post-structural model, like its predecessors, has been more successful than formalism in assigning characteristic aesthetic forms to non-aesthetic causes.

Yet the insights of Russian formalism remain persuasive: poetic language is contained within language, and the study of poetic language is essentially the study of language—its formal possibilities as well as its everyday practices. Similarly, the claim here is that human aesthetics is contained within the mechanics of a human sensorium and that the study of digital media aesthetics is essentially the study of the human neurological system, including those cognitive functions that process, interpret, and transform sensory data: semiosis.[13]

As early formalist theory evolved, there were attempts to develop theoretical positions encompassing both the universals of form and the variety of social structures that influence the effects of form.[14] Many of these attempts—structuralism, post-structuralism, hermeneutics, discourse analysis, social semiotics, and many other contemporary literary theories—apply early formalist methods toward an understanding of values and meanings within social and cultural contexts. However, early formalist theory seems, in retrospect, to extend more appropriately into cognitive science than into social science. In fact, if universal properties of human cognition operate in parallel with and reinforce formal characteristics of games and play, then there is much to be gained from pursuing a phenomenological hermeneutics in which the "interpretive community" guiding the values and meanings of digital media is precisely the biological origin and natural history of the human brain.

There is something quite humanistic in the claim that all humans possess, within their most basic perceptions and recognitions, the awe, the wonder, and the enlightenment associated with our most engaging forms of art. The function of art and literature is then to unravel these mysteries of the mind and the body: mysteries that are already, in the most basic sense, possessed. In contrast with this formalist point of view, contemporary cultural and critical studies often promote a seemingly more superficial and vague humanism, which must assume that the aesthetic properties of the human experience are found in the milieu of that experience rather than in the properties and mechanics of the human alone.

CHAPTER 4

Interface and Code

Play tends to remove the very nature of the mysterious.

—Roger Caillois, *Man, Play, and Games* (1961)

Poetics is the study of a particular sort of text. Aesthetics, on the other hand, is the study of a particular sort of human experience: pleasure—or, in the case of computer game play, the study of *fun*. Thus, unlike poetics, aesthetics requires some reference to the human senses (or sensorium) and that which enlivens or awakens or gives pleasure to the human sensorium.

Let's assume, as most do, that aesthetic pleasure results from a particular sort of art/text. If so, then when we focus a formalist discussion on the emotional effect—the pleasure—of that art/text, are we not committing what formalists called an "affective fallacy"? Are we not confusing the study of a work of art (e.g., poetics) with the study of the emotional/affective consequences of a work of art (e.g., aesthetics)?

After all, early formalists clearly attributed the functional consequence of *ostranenie* to poetic language. This seems to be an effect of poetic language. How can we not consider this sort of attribution an affective fallacy that turns our attention away from the form of art/text and toward the effects/consequences of art/text?

Two reasons. First, the formalist position assumes that the effect of poetic language is common and predictable—that is, that the function of poetic language has an objective nature independent of any idiosyncratic emotional response. And second and related, *ostranenie* does not affect the individual so much as it affects the raw senses of the species; this assigns a universal—even, in some ways, irresistible—quality to the poetic, subsequently provoking a particular, sense-based aesthetic response: a state of heightened awareness in which, according to Shklovsky, we "recover the sensation of life."

Thus, the study of art/text (e.g., poetics) becomes most critically the discovery and unraveling of forms of art/text that are most closely tied to the study of objective and universal pleasures of art/text (e.g., aesthetics).

Here, of course, I wish to explore what might be considered analogous to the pleasures of art/text: the pleasures of digital media and computer game play. One of the more obvious places to look for the root of these pleasures in new media is in the formal properties of new media *interactivity*—and the associated concept of immersion. Yet, while interactivity is probably the most oft-cited, most distinctive, and most influential component of new media, that term, like play, regularly eludes a precise definition.

Andersen,[1] for instance, prefers to locate interactivity in objective characteristics of computer-based signs—without much concern with either the interpretive values resulting from the interactive process or the pleasures that process might elicit. Similarly, Aarseth[2] defines new media interactivity as "ergodicity," which is understood as determined by the quantity of "reader" effort expended; again, this understanding is possible without any immediate concern with the consequential values (or pleasures) of reader effort expended.[3]

Neither of these two definitions of interactivity—nor many others available[4]—commonly couch interactivity within a functional biological context like that implied by Shklovsky and early formalists, wherein media interactivity is a formal characteristic transplanted from and reflecting fundamental properties of the human sensorium. When given such a biological origin, interactivity can be usefully understood as a human cognitive function prior to—and a necessary step toward—human semiosis. This then helps remove any theoretical disconnect between poetics and aesthetics, by connecting a particular form of art /text (poetics) with a particular and parallel form of pleasure (aesthetics).

I have previously weighed in on this matter of how best to conceptualize interactivity in *The Nature of Computer Games*, where I promote a definition of interactivity borrowed from Rafaeli and Sudweeks: interactivity "is the extent to which messages in a sequence relate to each other, and especially the extent to which later messages recount the relatedness of earlier messages."[5] Using this definition of interactivity, I have demonstrated how new media interactivity transforms signs and symbols in characteristic ways, focusing on and emphasizing their "relatedness."[6] This characteristic pattern of media interactivity entails a particular formal relationship among signs: a

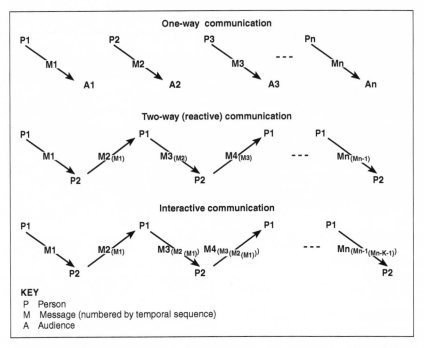

Figure 4.1. One-way, two-way, and interactive communication. Adapted from Rafaeli & Sudweeks (1997) [http://jcmc.indiana.edu/vol2/issue4/intctvty.gif].

temporal sequence of significations during which successive signs are used to construct a context within which subsequent signs are interpreted, valued, and given meaning. I call this relational process *recursive contextualization.* Let me break it down a bit further here. Recursive contextualization entails two important sub-processes: repetition and contextualization. Recursion, or self-reference, does not necessarily occur during repetition; nor is recursion necessarily a part of contextualization. Therefore, we can separate these two component processes—repetition and contextualization—and we can examine them individually during computer game play. Each is intimately associated with a specific element of computer game design and form that reflects the design and form of the human sensorium: interface and code.

THE COMPUTER GAME INTERFACE

Prototypically, computer games engage the human senses much more directly and immediately than do the genres of literature and art that Shklovsky and Wimsatt and other early formalists first analyzed. In fact, in most computer games—for example, first-person shooters—mastery of game mechanics and interface is a vital and necessary prelude to play. This is not a temporary impediment that is no longer important once overcome. Constant attention to and manipulation of game mechanics is required throughout computer game play, even when these requirements recede from the conscious awareness of players. In fact, game play is more enjoyable precisely when the attention to and manipulation of game mechanics recedes from conscious awareness and the player is fully engaged (or *immersed*) in the game. Therefore, it seems that one function of repetition in game play is to, over time, fully engage and thereby familiarize the senses, leading to a phenomenological state of "unawareness" or, in early formalist terms, *habituation*.

All computer games depend on a set of core sensory mechanics—similar in many ways to those of language and perception. These mechanics are habitualized, unconscious (i.e., capable of operating beneath surface awareness), and, like the fundamental characteristics of both language and perception, required prior to any subsequent aesthetic pleasure. Unlike the mechanics of language and perception, however, these mechanics are not solely embedded in the human body; they are, at least in part, embedded in the computer game interface.

One of the more striking characteristics of computer games is the extent to which these depend on and require some mastery of locomotor play prior to engagement with the game as a whole, particularly prior to engagement with game rules governing conceptual play. Of course, many generations of games have required similarly physical competencies: mumblety-peg, hop-scotch, and virtually all sports. However, few genres of games have maintained such obvious reliance on a ubiquitous mechanical "controller."

The evolution of the dedicated computer game controller—much like that of the equally common game interface of keyboard and mouse—has been relatively straightforward, deviating little from the simple toggles and control sticks of the 1970s to the more sophisticated, but otherwise quite similar, handheld devices of today. Computer game controllers have only occasionally employed mechanics beyond the conventional and consensual, or mechanics that strictly and realistically modeled their in-game referents. There are indeed computer game interfaces modeled as guns, steering wheels, skateboards, and guitars—for example, for the popular console game *Guitar Hero* (RedOctane, 2005). But these are, by and large, exceptions to the generic controllers used by the majority of games designed for Microsoft's Xbox, Sony's PlayStation, and, until very recently, Nintendo's dedicated game systems.[7]

And, significantly, despite ongoing innovations, all computer game controllers—including the Wii and other exceptions to current norms—have at least two common properties: (1) they employ arbitrary and simplified abstractions of their real-world referents, and (2) they require some level of habituation of response.

Player actions and choices within computer games are delayed, misapplied, and otherwise distorted—to the detriment of successful play—without a thorough and intuitive mastery of the game interface and controller. And, of course, learning to manipulate the computer game controller is a necessary (but only preliminary) stage of computer game play.

Habituation of response most often (though not always easily) comes through repetitive play, which computer games have in great abundance. This repetitive play integrates increasingly complex controller movements with more strategic and conceptual play. During this process, game instructions are learned so well as to require little conscious attention, and game rules come to dominate player awareness and decision making. Therein, computer game locomotor play is sublimated in service of conceptual play— a difficult and gradual task, which often only willing minds and nimble fingers are able to accomplish.

Significantly, while basic controller configurations are shared across games, the sequential patterns and manipulations required for advanced levels of computer game play are conspicuously unique. That is, while controller buttons have similar configurations patterned after the human hand,[8] new and different games always seem to require that these buttons be pushed in new and different ways. Even within games, there are many and different controller sequences to be mastered for many and different game processes. For this reason, each new computer game tends to evoke at least some portion of the habituation process anew, accompanied by similar requirements of recurring trials and errors, multiple saves and reloads. This phenomenon seems at first glance a barrier to computer game play (and subject to negative market pressures) and is all the more curious when innovative controller designs have little impact on the subjective experience of computer game play.[9]

Let us consider the interface of digital games analogous to the interface of the human body through which we gather, represent, and value our surroundings: the sensorium. Given an intractable sensorium, our senses are regulated by mechanics beyond our immediate control or awareness. While the computer game interface cannot entirely reconstitute the body in this exact way, it can do something parallel: it can reconfigure our interpretation of experience in order to prioritize—and de-prioritize—various aspects of that experience. By incorporating virtual valuations into the human experiential repertoire, computer games function simultaneously as experience simulators and as the experience being simulated. That is, the game interface mediates and, on occasion, substitutes for the embedded bodily mechanics of a human sensorium.

During computer game play, the domain of real-world experiences becomes a (relatively narrower) domain of virtual-world "immersions." These immersive virtual experiences become, once habituated, doppelgängers—parasitic on and indistinguishable from their non-virtual counterparts. The computer game interface evoking these "false" experiences has no ability to tag these experiences as true or false or in between. And, unlike the non-virtual experiences they emulate, these virtual experiences are not subject to any exterior (i.e., real-world) test of validity. Rather, their values are dependent on game code.

The entrenchment of these virtual experiences within computer game play is a function of repetition alone, which, in general and over time, tends to isolate habitualized behavior from its immediate surroundings. This process is similar, for instance, to how drivers constantly driving along the same route can eventually navigate that course without any conscious attention or concern for signs on the road. This habitualized activity (e.g., of driving) is then set apart from other, more willful behavior—at least until some anomalous sensation (an unexpected bump in the road) jolts us into a more active process of value determination. Until that moment, repetition of behavior is most likely to result in a decontextualization process, wherein habitualized behavior is isolated from other sensory concerns. This is precisely the function early formalists attributed to natural language use: we are so habitualized by natural language that we need poetic language (the occasional bump in the road) to restore a context in which we are alive, aware, and aesthetically stimulated.

Repetitive play in computer games, however, is part of a different formal context than repetitive use of a natural language.

THE COMPUTER GAME CODE

If computer game play were static, if it were not interactive in the "relatedness" sense of the earlier definition, then repetitive play would likely serve only habituation and decontextualization. However, computer game play is dynamic—particularly in its manipulation of semiotic form. This formal manipulation is guided and governed by the computer game code, which, regardless of its implementation, adheres to a recognizable pattern of construction and deconstruction. This code is then layered on top of the habituations of locomotor play, with a much different result than that of poetic language.

Computer game designs—and here I might even daresay *all* game designs—can be construed as the manipulation of arrays within a multidimensional matrix (or "space"). Commonly, these arrays are composed of seven values—plus or minus about two—despite the number of dimensions that may become subsequently involved. Among examples of this form, one of the clearest and most relevant to computer games is found in role-playing games, prototypically represented by Gary Gygax's *Dungeons & Dragons* (*D&D*) (originally published in 1974).

In *D&D*, for instance, character generation is based on selecting seven values (occasionally interrelated, occasionally not), with each value governing some portion of character behavior within the game's broader context. During play, these seven values function like a composite array (or vector)—valued in comparison with the arrays/vectors of other, similarly generated characters.[10]

This fundamental form of character generation is found in other games as well. All games modeling real-world objects—airplanes, pugilists, stockbrokers—represent these objects as aggregates of some limited (though sometimes quite large) number of "basic characteristics." In *D&D*, these characteristics are strength, intelligence, wisdom, dexterity, constitution, charisma, and comeliness, but in other games, these characteristics can be more abstract and/or more generic. (In many cases, for instance, the basic characteristics of a game object are representative values for that object's ingame virtual mass, volume, and/or velocity.)

We can now call contextualization this process of combining fundamental or "basic" characteristics into a game object with a single reference and value, for example, a player-character in *D&D*. This contextualization process is not limited to character generation alone but describes the creation of other game objects as well. For instance, in *D&D*, characters can be combined into teams, teams into adventures, and adventures into campaigns, so that each larger element of game play is formed through an aggregation of lower-level elements; and at each successive level, game rules govern how these nested combinations are valued in comparison with other, similar combinations.

Contextualization is actually only one of two important processes required by this particular game architecture. The other is opposition, which deconstructs, rather than constructs, game objects. After characters have been

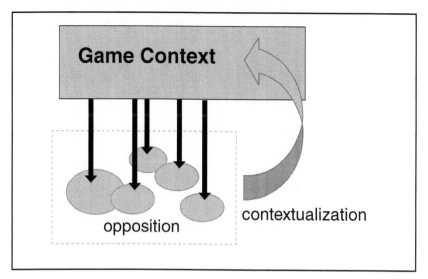

Figure 4.2. Common game functions of contextualization and opposition

created in *D&D*, for instance, their basic characteristics do not disappear but are called on from time to time, individually, by game rules. As I have explained in *The Nature of Computer Games*, whereas contextualization reveals similarities among game elements, opposition reveals differences among elements so that these elements can be valued, if needed, without reference to their immediate context.

In *Street Fighter II* (*SFII*), elements of content—Street Fighters, or officially, "World Warriors"—are valued in opposition to one another. These character-elements are composed of sub-elements (left kick, right kick, left punch, right punch, etc.), which are also valued in opposition to each other . . . These sub- and sub-sub-elements are the basic characteristics of each fighter-character; that is, all other characteristics of the Street Fighters (their names, clothes, coloring, etc.) are irrelevant to the mechanics of winning and losing the game and to the inner workings of the *SFII* game engine.[11]

Many other games replicate *Street Fighter II*'s architecture of opposition. Different characters and go-karts in *Super Mario Kart* are distinguished by basic characteristics of speed, acceleration, and handling ability. Planes in *Microsoft's Flight Simulator* have embedded basic characteristics representing the flight capabilities of real-world planes. The simple game objects of *Tetris*—falling rectangular blocks—have basic characteristics of length, width, and speed of descent. Characters in Will Wright's popular *Sims* series of games are composed of (up to) eight basic characteristics or "needs." Equally, squares on a *Monopoly* board are defined by a common set of basic characteristics: each square's position relative to the starting point of GO, its costs, its genre or class (real estate, railroad, chance, etc.), its in-game consequences, and so forth.

Importantly, contextualization and opposition have common properties across all games.[12] For instance, as regards contextualization, the same number of elements constitute game objects at the same contextual level; each of these elements has a finite range of values; each element value determines some, but not all, game consequences; and so forth. As regards opposition, game objects are given value only through opposition; opposition is a process activated, unlike contextualization, by player initiative and choice; oppositional values are only valid among objects at the same contextual level; and so forth.

These common features of game form seem to indicate that opposition and contextualization are operating at a relatively deep level of human cognition. In parallel, Lakoff and Johnson[13] have claimed that common features of natural language originate in those sensory processes associated with the positioning of material objects in relation to the human body in three-dimensional space. This deep structure is, for Lakoff and Johnson, apparent in the assignation (through metaphor) of "basic characteristics" of real-world objects to conceptual objects: a conceptual object's ability to "hold" other objects; whether or not that conceptual object is "pushable," "pullable," or "containable"; and so forth. Thus, not only do the referents of conceptual objects inhabit the natural world, but those basic characteristics—for example, pushable, pullable, containable—that assign those objects values within a natural language inhabit (or are embodied within) the natural world as well. This would seem to be even more the case as regards the basic characteristics and values of computer game objects.

Sometimes we refer to these sorts of "basic characteristics" in the natural world as "affordances,"[14] to emphasize their codependence on the human body and on the natural environment in which that human body has evolved. Computer games have numerous affordances of this sort: opportunities for action within the game environment, which are predisposed to be acted upon and to be valued—or to be "embodied"—in particular and predetermined ways. The simplest examples of these affordances are, of course, a reliance on bodily movements within the computer games: left, right, up, down, backward, forward.

The key here is that the computer game does not determine these opportunities and affordances so much as does the natural history of the game player—or, indeed, the natural history of the game player species. The game merely reproduces and replicates these opportunities—these affordances—in a repetitive and patterned way.

Our aesthetic response to the computer game, therefore, is bound by those embodied mechanisms that identify and respond to these affordances. Game designs are likewise more popular and appealing based on their ability to appease our natural inclinations to identify and respond to these affordances.

However, computer game players activate these embedded mechanisms in a virtual and, importantly, symbolic environment wherein those activations have different values and justifications than they do in the natural world. And, significantly, players are often most ingenious and most successful during play when they apply opportunities for contextualization and opposition in ways other than those intended—or allowed—by either the game design or by natural law. That is, because contextualization and opposition are such fundamental (and unavoidable) properties of cognition, players are only loosely bound in the use of these functions by game code.[15]

Within the game matrix, criteria of *winning conditions* establish a most desired game object, yet these conditions do not specify which combination of elements best (or only) meets those criteria. Finding and/or constructing a most desired game object—through successive applications of the embedded cognitive mechanisms of opposition and contextualization—is then the primary activity of game play, regardless of whether this activity takes place according to game rules or not.

During play, various combinations of elements are tried and tested, potentially involving, over time, all possible combinations within the game matrix. And once all possible combinations have been found (or "played"), the game becomes considerably less appealing. This is the fate, for instance, of games such as tic-tac-toe (naughts and crosses), which suffers from a relative lack of complexity in the number and combinations of its game elements.

The complexity of the oppositions and contextualizations required to win a game may vary significantly from game to game, but in each case, our earlier analogy remains apt: game elements analogous to arrays are manipulated within a multidimensional space composed of some limited number of basic characteristics established by the game design. The number of dimensions in this space—as well as the size of the arrays—is fixed both explicitly by game rules and implicitly by human cognition. Games that have an overly large and complex number of game elements are played more "poorly" by human players than those that do not. These more complex games are not unplayable by human players per se but are better played, for instance, by computer programs unburdened by common limitations of human cognition.

Consider checkers, for instance, as an example of a moderately complex game (more so than tic-tac-toe, at least)—determined by the number of player moves possible within any fixed game position or space. Also consider the still more complex—in this same sense—game of chess. The physical play space is superficially the same for checkers and chess (i.e., a sixty-four-square board), but the number of moves available to chess players within this "space" is much larger, and, correspondingly, the multidimensional matrix required to contain and adjudicate all these moves is much larger as well.

Computer programs are quite adept at playing checkers by considering all possible oppositional values of all possible moves: a strategy of "brute strength" that has proven competitively superior to human play. Chess-playing programs are becoming similarly adept, using primarily brute-strength techniques that (potentially) calculate every possible value of every possible array within the entirety of the game space. Thus, inside any sufficiently complex game—such as chess—human play is frequently insightful but less than optimum in generating the most desired game objects. Computer-based brute-strength strategies, on the other hand, seem less insightful than mysterious.

> [Deep Blue II] taught us nothing about human thought processes, other than that world-class chess-playing can be done in ways completely alien to the way in which human grandmasters do it.[16]

Yet these "alien" strategies prove, almost without exception, superior to human play in generating the most desired game objects—that is, in winning the game.

When human play is conceived in this manner—as an imperfect generative function testing all possible arrays within a fixed matrix—play can be understood to parallel other, similarly imperfect mechanisms that generate random variation and drive evolutionary change.[17] Therein, play, as a biological mechanic, may be better understood (and more fully realized) as a means of preserving (and transforming) the human species than as a means of pleasuring individual players.

Taken as a whole, multiple players and playings generate increasingly broader understandings and increasingly successful adaptations (measured both by knowledge gained and effects produced) within complex games—without being unnecessarily constrained, as artificial intelligence systems are, by the game code. This exploration, manipulation, and eventual mastery of the game system occurs despite (or perhaps because of) individual play being prone to frequent errors—for example, "blunders" in chess.

These errors and mistakes occur much more often in complex games than in non-complex games and can be seen as originating in the indiscriminate use of opposition and contextualization functions. That is, human play commonly fails to maintain the boundaries and rules of the game design. Realizing this, game designers make frequent use of the generative function of play during computer game "beta tests," which have become a vital part of the game design process, particularly for complex computer games, such as massively multi-player online role-playing games.

During MMO beta testing, individual players hammer away at the game and demonstrate how it might be "broken" in a variety of ways. During subsequent play beyond the beta testing period, individual players continue to explore the game space in ways often unforeseen by the game designers. This blustery and blundering sort of play may result in serendipitous "emergent" consequences,[18] but it more often simply results in some shortcut method of creating the game's most desired objects—including, of course, "cheating."

Thus, the game system can be seen as something of an ongoing struggle between the game code as law, which functions to restrict play, and play itself, which, largely through trial and error, tends to simplify and, if possible, unravel the game design in favor of some more human-compatible structure. Both sides in this struggle—game designers and game players—are bound by the same functions of contextualization and opposition. The game designer restricts the order and syntax of these functions,[19] while the game player is more prone to apply these functions indiscriminately, with little regard to their proper or intended use.

Individual play, in fact, seems characteristically unwilling—or perhaps simply unable—to exert precise control over contextualization and opposition. During play, these functions are applied to game elements at different contextual levels and out of logical sequence—again, in often seemingly random ways. Assigning game object values in such a willy-nilly fashion commonly results in paradoxes anathematic to the logical analysis of complex systems and is particularly destructive to those brute-strength algorithms so proficient at playing rigid-rule games, such as checkers and chess. Therein, in fact, lies a great deal of the ingenuity and uniqueness of human game play: its bull-in-a-china-shop approach and resulting blatant breaches of game rules.

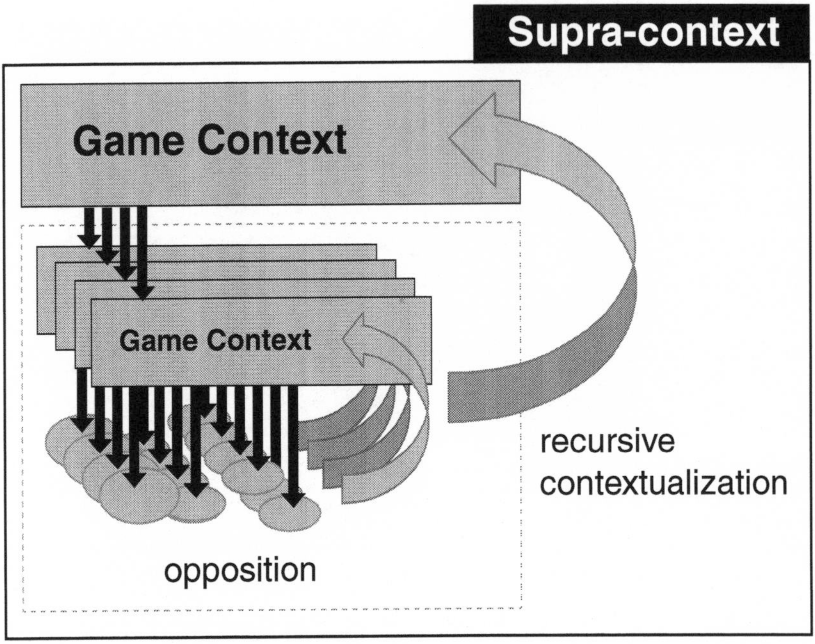

Figure 4.3. Transformative functions of play that create supra-contexts

Further, game play—and, again, this is particularly the case with computer game play—is characteristically repetitive. That is, game player choices—and the game contexts created by these choices—frequently become game elements (and sub-elements) within successive iterations of play, forming *supra-contexts* of play.

One of the more sophisticated and widely known implementations of this increasingly recursive pattern of play—and its supra-contextual consequences—is found in the *Civilization* series of games by Sid Meier and, later, Bruce Shelley. I have elsewhere explained the transformative elements of the "World Wonder" game elements in *Civilization*.[20] These elements transform the values of game elements—including themselves—and, during that transformation, likewise transform the game context that determines game values. This results in a self-referential form—a paradox—that is resolved only through repetitive play.

While *Civilization* is one of the more sophisticated and successful implementations of this particular form within a single-player game, most computer game designs display something similar in the construction of successive "levels" of player achievement, each resetting upon its completion to a nearly (though not quite) identical context.

Supra-contexts perhaps become most obvious during repeated play of cooperative (i.e., non-zero-sum) games, wherein self-reference becomes an important oppositional value governing subsequent play. This category of games includes the well-known prisoner's dilemma game, which, because of its relative simplicity and relevance to social contracts, has been analyzed in great detail. Here is the *Stanford Encyclopedia of Philosophy*'s description of the game:

> Tanya and Cinque have been arrested for robbing the Hibernia Savings Bank and placed in separate isolation cells. Both care much more about their personal freedom than about the welfare of their accomplice. A clever prosecutor makes the following offer to each. "You may choose to confess or remain silent. If you confess and your accomplice remains silent I will drop all charges against you and use your testimony to ensure that your accomplice does serious time. Likewise, if your accomplice confesses while you remain silent, they will go free while you do the time. If you both confess I get two convictions, but I'll see to it that you both get early parole. If you both remain silent, I'll have to settle for token sentences on firearms possession charges. If you wish to confess, you must leave a note with the jailer before my return tomorrow morning."[21]

The winning condition of the prisoner's dilemma game, as in all games, describes a most desired game object: the (least) amount of time spent in jail. As in other games, this most desired game object is composed of aggregate game elements—in this case, two: player 1's choice and player 2's choice. During repeated play, the outcomes of previous games become game sub-elements, affecting each player's choices in subsequent games. Linking a cascading series of game outcomes in this fashion creates, over time, a self-referencing form, which, something like mutually referencing cells in an Excel spreadsheet, would seem, on the surface, unstable, irresolvable, or both.

During the play process, however, players can, largely through trial and error (and something close to what is known, in artificial intelligence circles, as "backpropagation of error"),[22] discover things previously unknown about the game mechanics and structure. With that knowledge, players can produce a close approximation of the game's winning conditions for all involved. In the case of the prisoner's dilemma game, this approximation is a tit-for-tat strategy in which both players mimic the previous game choice of their opponent. This appears to be an objective or "natural" outcome of the game form that does not depend on anything other than an unwavering desire on the part of both players to win the game—and, of course, the ability of both players to vary their strategies over time: repetitive and recursive play.

It is important to note, however, that the paradoxical peculiarities of this recursive form entail that the game context can always be further altered. And this consequence, too, has been demonstrated during play of the prisoner's dilemma game. For instance, a group of researchers has successfully defeated the otherwise optimum tit-for-tat strategy in a tournament setting by manipulating the competitive game context in which tit-for-tat otherwise would emerge victorious.[23]

These researchers flooded the tournament with multiple tit-for-tat opponents, each of which competed rigorously against the tit-for-tat strategy and then colluded during competition with each other, in order to manipulate the tournament outcome in their favor. In fact, this same strategy of collusion within a presumptively competitive environment is found within online player-versus-player (PvP) play in MMOs as well. Computer game PvP players commonly trade wins back and forth and/or create dummy characters that absorb multiple losses, in order to manipulate and artificially increase their own win totals and related PvP rankings. Such is the curious and sometimes cruel function of a socially determined supra-contextualization of game rules: these tend to manipulate play contexts in characteristically non-egalitarian ways.[24]

Based on this realization, social constructivists have argued that games are, in fact, poorly understood using formalist analysis. This argument maintains that because games are subject to transformation through recursive contextualization—which can become, in social play contexts, socially determined—then it would follow that the games themselves are socially determined and subject to no formal rules other than, if any such exist, those rules governing the organization and sustenance of social order. However, social manipulations of game context—as in the prisoner's dilemma tournament previously described—do not transform the fundamental game forms that assure contextual transformation. These forms—opposition, contextualization, and, during repeated play, *recursive* self-reference—allow social manipulations to take place but are not themselves determined by social manipulations. Indeed, it seems more likely that the origin of these forms of game and play is located in biological necessity rather than in social convenience.

CHAPTER 5

The Computer Game Anti-aesthetic

We all need mirrors to remind ourselves who we are.
—Leonard Shelby, *Memento* (2003)

Recursive contextualization establishes the basis for a computer game aesthetic, or, perhaps better, an anti-aesthetic. This anti-aesthetic is an aesthetic of the psychophysical and, as such, borrows assumptions and claims from evolutionary psychology. For instance, the aesthetic of the anti would claim that the pleasures of sensation and semiosis are biologically determined and, for that reason, inextricably linked. These mechanics of sensation and semiosis, no doubt, have evolved to further the survival of the human organism, yet these mechanics, for all their usefulness, show gaps and flaws.

Piattelli-Palmarini (1994), for instance, has documented the degree to which human perception and judgment is consistently inaccurate in evaluating real-world events. Our perception—again, including perception, cognition, and semiosis as linked activities—invites a particular interpretation of the world due to its evolutionary design within a particular natural history. Real-world objects and events outside the physical and conceptual domain of our species remain alien to our senses and, correspondingly, alien to our minds. These invisible and mysterious domains may be as mundane as those portions of the electromagnetic spectrum beyond our natural vision or as exotic as quantum-level physics. We access such domains, if at all, through *anti*-intuitional means—for example, through some mechanical device substituting for natural perception (e.g., a radio telescope)—or, alternatively, through the formal abstractions of mathematics or some other, similarly nonlinguistic representational system. Thus, we might understand the form of alien domains through their analogous representation within our own personal domains, but the experience of these *other* domains remains apart from us, despite any ability we might discover to measure, manipulate, or otherwise control their presence and effects.

The psychophysical differs from the physical to the extent that it is a limited—and, because of its limitations, a distorted—subset of the physical. And those formal processes—sensation and semiosis—that construct the psychophysical laws governing our interpretive experiences are those same processes that guide interactive computer game play. Thus, computer game design and form is locked inside a particular and specific form of human representationalism, just as poetic language is locked inside a particular and specific form of natural language.

A computer game anti-aesthetic posits a formal and cognitive aesthetic, which, strictly speaking, reveals, rather than constructs, emotional response. This aesthetic is located in the interpretation and manipulation of symbolic form rather than in the assignation of any particular content, value, or meaning to that form. It is useful, then, to distinguish this position from others similar, which may recognize the same fundamental components of computer game play—that is, repetition, opposition, and contextualization—yet assign quite different (non-anti) functions to them.

Grodal (2000, 2003), for instance, has drawn a detailed comparison of the aesthetics of film and computer games, similar to that offered here.

> Video games provide an aesthetic of repetition, similar to that of everyday life . . . The video game experience is very much similar to . . . an everyday experience of learning and controlling by repetitive rehearsal . . . The end result of the learning process is what the Russian Formalists called *automation,* and what psychologists might call *desensitization by habituation.*[1] (italics in original)

Grodal's position, worth considering further, then goes something like this: the play of digital games is arousing. This arousal is cognitively labeled as specific emotional content according to the feedback players get from the game. And players are, to some important degree, in control of the feedback they get from the game. Therefore, Grodal claims that digital games as aesthetic experiences reproduce embedded, prelinguistic arousal patterns (including some narratives—or "meta-narratives"—importantly among these) and that, during play, players undergo "curiosity, surprise, suspense, and explorative coping" in response to these patterns. Repetitive play enables mastery of the game, but, more significantly, repetitive play allows players to learn and achieve emotional control. Thus, Grodal values the repetition of play primarily as a learning process accomplishing a specific function: emotional self-control.

This position is distinct from an anti-aesthetic insofar as it emphasizes the functional mastery of an emotional state. According to the model presented here, computer games and play evoke a distancing function (an anti-representational function), which "controls" emotions only insofar as it separates emotions (and all other things) from their common referents within conventional human experience.

The distinction of the anti-aesthetic is that, through self-reference and recursion, a formal process re-creates the form of real-world experience within the domain of self. If and when emotions (i.e., "content") become involved in this process, these emotions may be just as "real" as those accorded real-world experiences, yet the referents of those emotions will necessarily be something other than the real-world referents intended (by evolution and the natural history of the species).

For this reason, the computer game experience is both experience in the raw and, simultaneously, an active reinforcement of false experience.[2] Grodal seems to acknowledge the first portion of this claim but finds little reason to acknowledge or to assign any special relevance to the latter. In this, Grodal's position is similar to that of much of current game study, which locates and analyzes the message or meaning or theme of computer games in the same manner and according to the same aesthetic that those concepts are located and analyzed in film and other non-interactive media.

In a further instance, Aarseth (1999) has, in his analysis of the play of the first-person shooter *Doom*, identified two major tropes as "prenarrative master-figures of experience" (p. 39): aporia and epiphany. These arise from, respectively, an awareness of some obstacle or problem within the digital game and, subsequently, the revelation of its solution. Aarseth (1997) further locates these tropes within digital media in general or, in his terms, within "hypertext discourse" wherein aporia and epiphany together constitute a "fundamental layer of human experience" (pp. 91–92).

If we assign aporia the function of semiotic opposition, and if we assign epiphany the function of semiotic contextualization, then aporia and epiphany are closely analogous to similar concepts here. Yet, while Aarseth carefully distinguishes the aporia of hypertext from that associated with other, "anamorphic" forms, he clearly couches his aporia-epiphany pair within a literary context.

We then derive three categories: novels (in which we include Afternoon-type hyperfictions), anamorphic literature (solving enigmas), and metamorphic literature (the texts of change and unpredictability). The tigers that can be observed in the latter are unplanned, unbound, and untamed. But strangely, in these [latter] labyrinths, our influence as literary agents is much more real than in the two previous ones.[3]

According to an anti-aesthetic, of course, this latter claim simply cannot be true, since our influence as literary agents must depend on our natural language proclivities, which are trumped and subsumed and made inconsequential by the (anti-)experiential interface of repetitive and recursive computer game play.

When associating the mechanics of aesthetic response with the mechanics of language and literature (rather than with the mechanics of semiosis and experience), computer game aesthetics becomes a variant of media determinism in which the formal mechanics of interactive media (e.g., "hypertext discourse") substitute for those of natural language.

In contrast, an anti-aesthetic claims that the mechanics of aesthetic response are merely evoked through self-referral within the mechanics of digital media, which, in this function, precedes and transcends the more conventional domains of natural and poetic language. Thus, aporia and epiphany are not formally constructed during computer game design but merely revealed during computer game play—and can only be masked and distorted during any subsequent analysis of computer games as language-based aesthetic forms.

In summary, a computer game anti-aesthetic differs from conventional analysis of the computer game aesthetic in the former's emphasis of recursive contextualization and the psychophysical limitations of the experience of computer game play. Further, computer game play transcends poetic language and literature in its reference to broader and more fundamental bodily mechanics associated with interpretive experiences.

Perhaps the greatest advantage of an anti-aesthetic in this regard is that it more readily includes and explains those experiences associated with computer game play that are considered risky, harmful, against the rules, or in some other way bad. Indeed, within an anti-aesthetic, "bad" play becomes exemplary play. This bad play includes all emotions and efforts expended prior to Grodal's sense of mastery and/or prior to Aarseth's state of epiphany: frustration, isolation, obsession, self-immersion, defeat. While conventional aesthetic analysis discounts, considers incomplete, or otherwise ignores these emotions and efforts, the anti-aesthetic considers them common, central, and generative.

Computer game play is an experience in which the liminal—determined by a particular formal relationship among computer game objects and values—is given a bodily component and cause that, in that process, viscerally confirms the play experience. What seems to be becomes, in the computer game, what is; and the psychophysical is therein asserted and confirmed as the physical. This confirmation is normally a temporary state, undermined not only by the fragile and fleeting nature of play itself but also by the dialectical relationship between the experience of the computer game as simulation and the experience of the computer game as self.

Computer game designers have tended to extend the experience of the liminal within computer games—commonly as an endless series of goals or levels—wherein players oscillate between neophyte ("newbie") and expert. Expert status is achieved with full and thorough knowledge of computer game object-value relationships and with the corresponding assimilation of those relationships at some habituated and visceral level. Because of this latter requirement, full and thorough *knowledge* of game mechanics is not alone sufficient to locate and produce the computer game aesthetic. Full and thorough knowledge is more equivalent to what is required during the aesthetic experience of reading text—and might be similarly claimed, for instance, from a full and thorough reading of computer game rules, from a full and thorough reading of other computer game players' accounts of their play, or from a full and thorough knowledge of computer game *interface* and computer game *code*. But none of these, in isolation, is sufficient.

Computer game players eschew rules manuals in favor of an immediate experience, and many game designs—MMOs among them—no longer, if they ever did, publish game manuals in anything close to complete form. Knowledge of the computer game experience is acquired only through the immediate and the direct, grounded only through the senses. This is not dissimilar from the knowledge of the warmth of the sun or the knowledge of riding a bike or the knowledge of some other intimate and personal kinesthetic joy. As such, this knowledge heralds, perhaps, a burgeoning aesthetic of the haptic senses, evoked not by individual sensations per se but by their sequential presentation within an interactive and artificial (and therein abstract and symbolic) environment. Play would therein be instrumental in forging a relationship among our senses, our environment, and the neurological systems that mediate the two.

In art, as in play, something comes into presence that has never been there before; the work is made present, presented, through play.[4]

Perhaps peekaboo, more than any novel or film, is the quintessential computer game, alternating between our expectations and realizations at such a visceral level that the culminate pleasure of the game lies most fundamentally in the realization that it is false. Furthering this analogy, peekaboo is also a game that can be wholly enacted by the self, with the reward of a familiar face provided as easily by a mechanical interface—for example, a video display—as by the physical presence of another human being: peekaboo in a mirror.

When the psychophysical—our perception of self—is asserted and confirmed during computer game play, there is nothing to deny it other than some grotesque failure of the game mechanics (e.g., a power outage) or, through purposeful design, the end of the game. In the natural world, play provides a means to deny and therein explore the boundaries of our environment and our selves, yet these remain unassailably physical boundaries. There are no analogous physical boundaries—other than, perhaps, the physical exhaustion of the computer game player—delimiting play within a virtual world. In the natural world in which our bodies and our play have evolved, experience is available to trump belief. In the virtual world of the computer game, belief is given its own body of experience.

Insofar as computer game play evokes a private experiential ground, there is little ability to either differentiate or choose between what seems to be and what is. And, in fact, given the choice, computer game players much seem to prefer what seems to be. In granting this preference, computer games function as a means of *anti*-control, a conscious—or at least willful—attempt to lose consciousness, to disregard the sensation of *other* in favor of a more direct and immediate engagement of body and mind and the sensation of *self*.

Patterned after our own sensory mechanisms (a human sensorium) and those cognitive adaptations that have resulted in knowing the world through representations (a human semiosis), computer games appear capable of extending human knowledge only to the extent that human experience can be *represented*. During computer game play, representations of human experience—histories, narratives, societies, and simulations—are equally hollowed by the habitual and repetitive nature of play and are equally transformed by a more fundamental, proto-representation: an *anti*-form. Computer game play then serves as a revelation of those natural and historical affordances that determine our behavior and, simultaneously, for better or worse, as a means to avoid those determinations.

CHAPTER 6

Anti-narrative

> Media cannot change our innate cognitive and emotional archi-
> tecture, only invent products that may activate and enhance the
> innate specifications.
>
> —Torben Grodal, *Stories for the Eye, Ear, and Muscles* (2003)

In the late 1800s, railroads were "iron horses." In the early 1900s, automo-
biles were "horseless carriages." And in the late 1900s, computer games were
"interactive fictions."

From a contemporary perspective, it is no doubt difficult to imagine the
importance of the horse within pre-industrial society. And, currently, there
is little doubt about the importance of fiction and narrative in contemporary
society. The importance of the horse and the importance of narrative fiction,
however, are on similar and diminishing trajectories.

While the term *fiction* certainly has more generic uses, we have come to
associate it with prose narrative. And the form and fate of fiction, as prose
narrative, are tightly linked to the form and fate of text. Narrative, however,
has more general functions that are neither necessarily nor inextricably
linked to prose form. Cognitive psychologists identify narrative as a particular style of thinking/learning—sometimes explicitly,[1] sometimes less so.[2] In
developmental theories of learning, a narrative mode of thinking commonly
occurs—in children, for instance—prior to some more "advanced" mode
(e.g., a more abstract/formal mode of thinking).

Recent cognitive theory recognizes both the persistence and the intrac-
tability of narratives within human cognition.[3] William Labov, a linguist, has
compiled universal features of narratives;[4] in brief, Labov and others[5] consider narrative as *a folk theory of causes.* That is, stories in general—and narratives in particular—function as sense-making devices by providing explicit

and causal relationships among otherwise unrelated observations: a temporal sequencing of events.

Thus, narratives are a sort of semiotic template, recording and communicating the results of some previously completed human meaning-making process. In computer game play, however, the human meaning-making process is never previously completed but always presently ongoing. Therefore, narratives—and particularly prose narratives—often function in conflict with an aesthetic of play.

ANTI-NARRATIVE

Roman Jakobson was one of the youngest of the early Russian formalists and a member of the original group who proved most facile in applying formalist principles and techniques within other theoretical disciplines. Also one of the founders of the Moscow Linguistic Circle, Jakobson made multiple contributions to linguistics and literary theory. Most pertinent here is Jakobson's classification of literary genres on the basis of their characteristic tropes or, put more generally, characteristic relationships among signs.

Whereas I have previously classified semiotic processes as either oppositional or contextual, Jakobson establishes a similar binary division within human semiosis, marked by "selection" and "combination."[6] Jakobson argues, in formalist fashion, that broader literary forms are derivative of these two most basic and fundamental forms. Jakobson associates "selection" with metaphor and, at the level of genre, with romanticism; he associates "combination" with metonymy and, at the level of genre, realism.

It is easy to find parallels between Jakobson's analysis, my own, and that of contemporary computer game critics such as Espen Aarseth, who identifies two formal "master tropes" characterizing not only all computer game play but all "hypertext discourse."[7] In parallel with early formalist claims, Aarseth's tropes display distinct phenomenological effects. The first is *aporia*, a feeling of confusion or helplessness among players—a state associated with the initial awareness and processing of oppositional signs such as those confronted during initial exposure to the physical interface of action/arcade games or, as Aarseth notes, during encounters with difficult puzzles or major obstacles within any game. The second of Aarseth's master tropes is *epiphany*, resulting from the resolution of oppositions (and, thus, the resolution of aporia) through a contextualization process.

Further, Aarseth classifies his tropes as "pre-narrative," existing apart from (or at least prior to) those semiotic processes associated with language and literature. Similarly, Jakobson's analysis implies that while metaphor is fundamentally an intra-linguistic form, metonymy is *meta-lingual*. From this, we then must assume that any formal analysis regarding such forms must also be meta-lingual as well.

My own analysis concurs with this line: that there exists both a formal and affective distinction between poetic form and computer game form; that this formal and affective distinction establishes the interactive aesthetic form as the more fundamental form (e.g., as either supra- or meta-lingual in nature); and that this interactive form has, as one of its major consequences, what early formalists referred to as a habituation of the senses. I would, in fact, argue even the stronger position that, as a result of the preceding, narrative forms are incongruous and frequently dysfunctional when applied within interactive computer game designs.

Jakobson believed we could learn more about the nature of language from its limitations (e.g., those observed in aphasia patients) than from its achievements; likewise, we may well learn more about the nature of digital media from its failed appropriations of literary forms—stories and narratives—than from its widespread depiction as "interactive fiction."

PLAY IN TEXT

One of the better-known and more-accomplished demonstrations of play with narrative is found in the work of Jorge Luis Borges, who, within traditional literary forms (e.g., the short story "Funes the Memorious"), describes semiotic processes I have closely associated with play. One is boundless *opposition*.

> Funes . . . was, let us not forget, almost incapable of general, platonic ideas. It was not only difficult for him to understand that the generic term dog embraced so many unlike specimens of differing sizes and different forms; he was disturbed by the fact that a dog at three-fourteen (seen in profile) should have the same name as the dog at three-fifteen (seen from the front) . . . He was the solitary and lucid spectator of a multiform world which was instantaneously and almost intolerably exact.

Another is limitless *contextualization*.

> The voice of Funes, out of the darkness, continued . . . The first stimulus to his work, I believe, had been his discontent with the fact that "thirty-three

Uruguayans" required two symbols and three words, rather than a single word and a single symbol. Later he applied his extravagant principle to the other numbers. In place of seven thousand thirteen, he would say (for example) Máximo Perez; in place of seven thousand fourteen, The Train; other numbers were Luis Melián Lafinur, Olimar, Brimstone, Clubs, The Whale, Gas, The Cauldron, Napoleon, Agustín de Vedia. In lieu of five hundred, he would say nine. Each word had a particular sign, a species of mark; the last were very complicated.

Another is paradoxical *recursion*.

In effect, Funes not only remembered every leaf on every tree of every wood, but even every one of the times he had perceived or imagined it. He determined to reduce all of his past experience to some seventy thousand recollections, which he would later define numerically. Two considerations dissuaded him: the thought that the task was interminable and the thought that it was useless.

Yet it remains Funes the character who plays, and it remains Borges the author who describes and translates that play into narrative form. Likewise, all similar forays into the un- and anti-conventional within narrative are translations within that narrative form[8]—unless or until these become something *else*, either something untranslatable entirely or something other than narrative: for example, "mysticism" (Blake), "philosophy" (Nietzsche), "madness" (Blake, Nietzsche, Kafka), or some other.

Indeed, "poetic" language itself can be considered an excursion into a sort of linguistic "madness," in which words and meanings range—sometimes uncontrollably and unpredictably—beyond their conventional use. However, the inability of play in language—even poetic language—to completely escape the form of language means that the relationship between the computer game player and digital code is ultimately quite different from the relationship between the reader of literature and the "code" of language.

Literature remains most essentially a process of communication in which meanings and values are transmitted (or shared, if you prefer) from person to person through a common language/code system that is, importantly, grounded in human experience. In contrast, during computer game play, meanings and values are neither definitively made nor permanently grounded.

Certainly, computer game code is bound to some degree by the rules of the game, but during play, computer game players both abide by and, on a frequent and regular basis, test, revise, and break the rules. Much computer game play is motivated by a sense of mastery over and movement beyond the rules: bad play. Any similar "movement beyond" the code of language would quickly render natural language—along with the poetic language that resides within it—meaningless.

Within the rules of language, narratives bind, restrict, and motivate the experience of reading. The "rules" of digital code have no similar impact on the experience of play. Computer game design may well incorporate (simulate) literary functions, but these cannot serve the same function as literature insofar as these functions are rules of a game. For, once part of the rules of a game, the rules of language must submit to the same process of play and semiotic transformation as all other parts of the game: they must and will be breakable.

For this reason, computer games using the rules of language as a design element—notably so-called interactive fiction—have found it extremely difficult to combine the distinct aesthetics of literature and play. Critics now recognize the dissonance of these respective forms but do not therein acknowledge their fundamental incompatibility. Montfort,[9] for instance, describes interactive fiction designs as only "potential" narratives (yet narratives nonetheless); similarly, the literary-inspired analysis of Ryan[10] emphasizes the use of narrative patterns and processes within interactive digital media to generate, for instance, a variety of "possible worlds." In such analysis, the question remains whether the semiotic process necessary to generate potentials and possibilities is not antithetic to the semiotic process necessary to construct and interpret narratives.

While poetic language reveals the underlying mechanics of an embodied language, computer games and other playfully interactive digital media forms reveal only the contents—the *emptiness*—of a disembodied semiosis.

HYPERTEXT

It may be useful here to compare the experience of playing a game with the experience of reading a peculiarly game-like text: hypertext. Aarseth has described the experience of hypertext reading as an "ergodic" art form driven by aporia and epiphany, two concepts he also closely associates with computer game play.

The aporia-epiphany pair is thus not a narrative structure but constitutes a more fundamental layer of human experience, from which narratives are spun.[11]

I have described here (and elsewhere)[12] a similar dialectic resulting from the formal opposition and subsequent contextualization of signs, involving Spencer-Brown's "mark of distinction" and the dissolution of this mark during its reapplication to itself. However, that description is a bit different from that implied by aporia and epiphany, even though both descriptions seem to refer to a similar, fundamental form.[13]

Aarseth describes properties of the experience of hypertext reading from a reader's perspective and as these are guided by that reader's interpretive processes, often with narrative as a guide and goal. Here, I am maintaining that the dialectical properties of the anti-form of play lie in the form of play itself—without any goals other than those goals embedded within and required by that form. Interactive media—most particularly computer games—reproduce this form most closely, but it is shared in part by the digital mechanics of hypertext as well. This peculiar form consists of a peculiar set of relationships between: (a) objects and values (as maintained by the computer game code) and (b) the local and habituated responses necessary to access and assimilate those object-value relationships (as maintained by the computer game interface).

The resulting anti-form may be collapsed through full knowledge of game rules and outcomes (the culminating result of the simulation, wherein all object-value relationships are fully disclosed) or through lack of player interest or investment in game rules and outcomes (e.g., during either the detached reverie of the daydreamer or the purposeful misdirection of the cheater). In the first instance, object-value relationships are made too strict; in the second instance, those relationships are made too loose. In between is where computer game play, as a unique aesthetic form, resides.[14] Hypertext, as an intermediary between text and game, allows the reader to manipulate (or play with) object-value relationships, but it does not, as computer games do, confirm and validate that play within a bodily mechanic.

Over time, because of the mechanical necessities of computer game hardware (and the consensual social necessity of a common set of game rules), computer games have tended to culminate more often in the simulative than in the selfish. This simulative structure often takes a recognizably narrative form in which computer game players do not doubt or destroy but only, on occasion, intervene—in a fashion similar to how readers intervene during the experience of hypertext reading. In such circumstances, social rules often come to promote and enforce a limited set of player interventions, and playing computer games becomes, like reading hypertext can become, a derivative process: a derivation and simulation of reading text.

ANTI-FILM

There is now a growing body of criticism that compares the aesthetics of digital games to the aesthetics of film[15] and, related, to the broader category of visual aesthetics.[16] And rightfully so—since, of all media arts, film and computer games seem, at least superficially, most closely related.

Film—particularly commercial movies—is a closer aesthetic analog to popular computer games than is prose fiction. This is perhaps more obvious during computer game design than during computer game play. Both aesthetic forms—games and movies—follow similar designing, storyboarding, production, and building processes; and both share (and, in fact, require) similar artists, skills, and aesthetic values.[17] As a result of this shared design process, both sets of designs as built—movies and games—display similar forms and structures.

In order to consider film as a sort of anti-process like play, consider the typical context within which the signs and symbols of film are experienced. A related complex of psychoanalytical, illusion, and "dream" theories of film[18] emphatically reference the consistent placement of film audiences in a theater in which the material body (the human sensorium) is isolated, deprived, numbed, and, in effect, desensitized.

> Morin and Mitry also described the spectatorial condition as a para-oneiric state. For the former, this condition is produced by several factors: the darkness of the auditorium; the comfort of the chair, which induces the spectator to relax and fantasise; the passivity and absence of movement, inviting a psychic and emotive participation. In such a regressive state, according to Morin, the spectator increases the normal psychic mechanisms of projection and identification, and somehow fulfils her or his most intimate desires. For Mitry, the spectatorial state lies somewhere between dream and daydream. In fact, it is similar to dreams in that the imaginary replaces the real; and it resembles daydreaming because the spectator always preserves a certain consciousness.[19]

Under such conditions, film functions somewhat analogously to natural and poetic language. That is, film images are conveyed within an anti-experiential context emphasizing the interpretive component of representations while, simultaneously, damping the conventional visceral responses associated with the referents of those representations. The on-screen images then recall experience through reference rather than through reproduction. When we react to darkness within a film, for instance, we are reacting to the image or representation of darkness on the screen. The darkness in the theater, meanwhile, does not affect us in a similar way; that is, the darkness in the theater is just as required and just as common when viewing bright and sunny scenes on film.

A film audience's "para-oneiric"[20] state avoids the interruptions of—or mediates—more natural, immediate, and conventional perception. Within such a state, any willing suspension of disbelief accorded to the film's narrative is reinforced by an accompanying involuntary state of sensory deprivation. With bodily senses disengaged, human semiosis becomes more focused, able, and likely to engage perception as an interpretive (rather than as a responsive or an interactive) activity—that is, as within a dream.

In disassociating the perception of films from the experience of bodies, film recalls and calls into question the embedded conventions and mechanics of our human visual representational system, or, we might say, the film calls into question our habitualized perceptual "language." In this sense, film can be labeled a form of anti-perception. In the context of perception, we call such anti-perceptions illusions. In the context of interpretations and meanings, we call such representations paradoxes.

Conventional film content is structured in a manner enhancing the aesthetic experience of the medium and, simultaneously, distinguishing that experience from a more raw and unmediated perception. Virtually all film editing demonstrates and relies on the disassociation of perceptual stimulus from experiential moment. Cuts, fades, and dissolves assume some advanced (and learned) level of cognitive processing beyond that of natural perception; and such artificial visual devices then become metaphors (rather than reproductions) of the perceptually literal.

Following this line of thought, we might assume that any visual sign or symbol in film that too closely evokes the experience of its real-world referent would have a dissonant aesthetic effect—similar to that of breaking the fourth wall in a theatrical production. Two representative examples come to mind. The first is the long-imagined ideal of three-dimensional film. Due to technical difficulties, the 3-D film is currently discounted as an aesthetic medium and relegated to documentary or novelty (i.e., thrill-seeking) use. However, even given some future, less cumbersome implementation, 3-D displays may narrow the aesthetic possibilities of film for formal reasons.

Images within film that cause us to respond to them as experiential objects—that is, images that are interpreted as the thing itself rather than as a representation of that thing (i.e., images as icons)—limit and detract from the interpretation of those images within the dream-like or illusionary state of the moviegoer. This is even true of realistically colored images, which, as the colorization controversy in the film industry has demonstrated, potentially interfere with director intentions, film themes, or other similar cognitive overlays—including narrative templates. This is certainly true of certain types of on-screen characters and characterizations—such as those employed by professional wrestling (or "rassling") events—which blur the distinction between representation and reality at the cost of interpretive nuance and cognitive depth.

Still another obvious example of iconic dissonance in film is pornography, which engages the mechanics of perception more immediately and directly than conventional film aesthetics allow. For this reason, pornographic images have predictably disruptive effects on the cognitive and interpretive processes associated with and enjoyed within more conventionally "serious" films.[21]

In film, overly realistic and iconic images take on the accoutrements of spectacle and most often first masquerade as experience in the raw—as did, according to most popular accounts, the Lumiere brothers' well-known scene of a train pulling into the Ciotat station (1895). The degree to which this masquerade might be subsequently penetrated is determined by the degree to which the film images can be disassociated from their real-world referents and reinterpreted within the confines of some semiotic template—a grammar or film "language," for instance—distinct from that of human perception.

In most commercial digital games, the same sort of "seriousness" we have come to associate with films as "works of art" is absent and, in most cases, detrimental to the enjoyment of play. In fact, verisimilitude—the domain of the iconic—is in great demand within digital games, where digital images and representations increasingly border on the simulative.

While perceptual novelties within film remain largely theme-park-like distractions, digital games revel in such novelties and have quickly found ways to incorporate them into conventional game designs. Sensory feedback, for instance—the vibration function of game controllers—is now standard fare in console games; and the context in which digital games are played is likewise more arousing, interactive, and accepting of extraneous stimuli—for example, music and conversation—than the dark dream tank of the movie theater. In fact, it is difficult to think of any formal representation—iconic or not, pornographic or not—that would have a disruptive effect on game aesthetics and play. For, during play, disruption—the continuous introduction of novelty—is, in a sense, the whole point.

PLAY IN FILM

The conventional movie is much more narrowly confined than the conventional computer game regarding, in particular, *time*.[22] For instance, the average length of a commercial Hollywood movie has varied over its history but is decidedly under three hours. The average play of a digital game, on the other hand, despite a great deal of variation, is far, far beyond three hours. Therefore, within the limited amount of time movies engage their viewers, there is simply less time available for play and any related anti-nesses. Nevertheless, some films and filmmakers display a playfully destructive intent—and the makeup of these displays is telling.

Groundhog Day (Ramis, 1993), for instance, is a well-known and popular movie that, in a sense, "destroys" conventional time by looping its characters through the same twenty-four hours of a single Groundhog Day. Time travel, repetition, and recursion are, of course, frequent themes in otherwise conventional narratives—particularly within science fiction and fantasy genres. These subjective distortions of "normal" time are commonly dealt with, as they are in *Groundhog Day,* through the lens of a single character who experiences those distortions within a conventional chronological sequence—that is, within the context of a conventional narrative and its narrator. In *Groundhog Day,* Phil Conner's (and our) point of view is quite straightforward and linear, despite all the fragmentation, repetition, recursion, and multiple destructions going on in and about the movie's fictional version of Punxsutawney.

More obviously game-like in form and, correspondingly, more playful in its destruction of the conventional is *Lola Rennt,* or *Run Lola Run* (Tykwer, 1998). The visual context of *Run Lola Run,* marked as much by its style as its substance, is clearly *anti*-real. The movie is played to a virtually continuous techno-beat; the cast is distinguished more by their 3-D, rotating, graphic-cardish, cartoon-inspired profiles than by their dialog; and bits of self-conscious animation and other digitized embellishments dot the rendering of Lola's hometown. And, of course and most significantly, there is the triple repetition of Lola's run through town, which substitutes for a conventional plot and offers the movie's most blatant destruction of time and space.

Run Lola Run repeats the same sequence of events—with minor alterations that give these repeated scenes increasingly recursive value—until Lola and her boyfriend reach a happy ending. The first two sequences end, first, with the death of Lola and, second, with the death of her boyfriend. Finally, the movie reloads a third time and, from Lola's point of view, starts anew. From the audience's point of view, of course, this third time is not truly the new but rather the charm; for, suddenly, we are left at movie's end with the pop quiz of a narrative.

The narrative of *Run Lola Run*—its folk theory of causes—would seem to be that persistence (or perhaps true love) alters the otherwise inevitable narrative of history. The movie's keynote sequence comes during its third and final repetition, when Lola enters a casino and, through sheer force of will, overcomes chance and chaos, reasserts order, and walks out with her happy ending. This denouement strongly recalls a similar resolution within *Groundhog Day:* love conquers all, including destructions of play. However, in *Run Lola Run,* without the helpful overlay of *Groundhog Day*'s more conventional narrative, the lesson learned requires a bit more effort on the part of the viewer.

Run Lola Run is, in this sense, more "ergodic"[23] than *Groundhog Day.* Yet *Run Lola Run* culminates in little more than fifty-two pickup: a gamelike form with the accoutrements but not the essence of play. The movie's narrative is then a sort of inside joke about game play, a sleight of hand and eye that erases both the death of its protagonist and the seriousness of its experience. If *Groundhog Day* is a movie of false time, then *Run Lola Run* is likewise a movie of false play. For in both movies, the final scenes break all spells, dispel all magics, and end all plays.

Memento (Nolan, 2000) is a third example of cinematic playfulness that stretches a bit further into the realm of *anti. Memento* tells the story of Leonard Shelby, who is afflicted with short-term memory loss. Leonard can't remember anything that happens much beyond thirty seconds ago, and so his life is a series of continuously novel thirty-second sequences.

Leonard manages this condition by leaving his newly regenerated thirty-second self notes written and Polaroids taken by his previously generated thirty-second selves. If Leonard has something really important to say to his future, he tattoos it on his chest. The movie communicates Leonard's state by showing Leonard's actions in reverse order so that, like Leonard, the audience doesn't know what or which came first—until the end of the movie, when, unlike Leonard, the audience finally gets to remember the whole thing.

Memento, in comparison to our first two examples, is unique in that the viewer's experience of structures—and structuring—is itself distorted. Our experience of Leonard's situation is, as a result, more immediate and in parallel with his own. In *Groundhog Day,* our knowledge of Phil Connor's narrative perspective serves as interpretive guide. In *Run Lola Run,* our knowledge of movies and movie forms—and games and game forms—serves as an interpretive map. In *Memento,* our interpretations are thwarted. In order to view the movie normally, we must view it abnormally: we must inspect our own knowledge—our own mind, memory, and expectations—which, like Leonard's, are made suspect.

And what cinematic form, exactly, brings us to these playful moments of self-doubt?

> Once you see "Memento" a couple of times, you figure out the devilish scheme Nolan has constructed . . . If we give letters to the backward color scenes and numbers to the monochrome scenes, then what Nolan presents us with is this: Credits, 1, V, 2, U, 3, T, 4, S, 5, R, 6, Q . . . all the way to 20, C, 21, B, and, finally, a scene I'm going to call 22/A . . . So, if you want to look at the story as it would actually transpire chronologically, rather than in the disjointed way Nolan presents it . . . you would watch the black-and-white scenes in the same order (1 to 21), followed by the black-and-white/color transition scene (22/A). You would then have to watch the remaining color scenes in reverse order, from B up to V, finishing with the opening credit sequence, in which we see Teddy meet his maker at Leonard's hands: 1, 2, 3, 4, 5, 6, 7, 8, 9, 10, 11, 12, 13, 14, 15, 16, 17, 18, 19, 20, 21, 22/A, B, C, D, E, F, G, H, I, J, K, L, M, N, O, P, Q, R, S, T, U, V.[24]

This scheme may be "devilish," but it is otherwise quite patterned and not, in fact, overly difficult to achieve or decode. And yet such a seemingly mechanical presentation of events—a mere reversal of order—has a significant impact on our viewing experience. For *Memento* is designed not to create but to destroy. And its destruction is quite pointed at preexisting structures of mind, memory, cognition, and self.

Playful art—and *Memento,* much more than our two previous examples, falls into this category—is *self*-reflective, in both senses of "self." That is, play is self-reflective in that it refers to and represents its own form, its own play; our experience in viewing *Memento,* for instance, is as much about our own mental form as it is about the movie's culminate form. Further, play is self-reflective in that, in referring to and representing its own form, it simultaneously and analogously refers to and represents the cognitive processes that build and structure the human condition we characterize as "self."

This latter sense of "self" is a difficult form to recognize because it conflates playful context with playful process. However, just as a simulation of a simulation is both a representation of that thing it represents (a simulation *of*) and, simultaneously, the thing itself (a *simulation* of), those cognitive processes that refer to themselves are both references to play and play itself. Or, put more simply, play is fundamentally *selfish*—and so is *Memento*. And Leonard's peculiar mental state is a formal characteristic of all similarly anti-aesthetic (or selfishly playful) forms.

A great many digital adventure games, for instance, are designed around problems associated with a Leonard-like memory deprivation. Indeed, in such games there always seems to be a Leonard-like character who doesn't know who (or what) he is, or a robot that has had its memory wiped, or something similar. And then the whole purpose (or theme, or narrative) of these games is to recover missing information. This particular formal structure— often realized as a detective/mystery story, or, more generally, as a traversing of the labyrinth[25]—appears again and again as a common narrative template in digital games (the *Zork* series, *Myst*, *Knights of the Old Republic*, etc.). But this template is not limited to adventure games per se. It re-appears during all applications of narrative within digital media that are increasingly interactive and increasingly susceptible to free play.

> We could say that the three classic hypertexts, Michael Joyce's *Afternoon*, Stuart Moulthrop's *Victory Garden*, and Shelley Jackson's *Patchwork Girl* all did what they could to make the reader more receptive to the marvels of their labyrinths: by using hidden and conditional links to highlight and parallel the defences and self-denials of the protagonist in *Afternoon*, his general unwillingness to know; evoking and concretising the familiar literary tradition of forking paths of Borges, Coover and Pynchon in *Victory Garden;* and foregrounding Frankensteinian bodily metaphors to ease the postmodernist butchery work of connecting parts and wholes in *Patchwork Girl.*[26]

When game play is structured by narrative (or by *time*), that play is forced to adopt a traversing-the-labyrinth path. There is something missing; the player has to find it, recover it, and use it to make sense of whatever the player is doing; and then—well, then the game ends. That is, the value of whatever the player is playing with has already been valued by the narrative, and further play does not—cannot—change that value. The player, caught within these *other* values, can only walk through a series of paint-by-number, dance-hall steps prepared and structured by a preexisting and forever invulnerable *other.* Just as Lola runs through her town. Just as Leonard stumbles through his movie.

Inside *Memento,* Leonard is living inside a digital adventure game. But unlike when Lola or you or I play our games, Leonard isn't limited to recovering missing information lost; he—and he alone—gets to make meanings new.

The notes and Polaroids Leonard sends himself form scattered and broken narratives (some false, some true), which, as much in their absence as their presence, drive Leonard to solve the puzzles of his narrative-imposed memory loss. By the end of the movie, Leonard manages to thwart those non-memory-impaired folk—including all narrators and their narrations—who are using his condition for their own ends. The will and purpose of the self, Leonard's actions show us, are more fundamental than those otherwise arbitrary narratives that deny the will and purpose of the self.

And how does Leonard show us this? It's a difficult demonstration, to be sure—an almost self-contradictory and paradoxical demonstration in that Leonard finds himself irrevocably caught, as is the viewer, within the larger context of movie and narrative.

Yet Leonard denies. He resists; he destroys; he murders. He kills. In *Memento,* there is a carefully plotted structure to Leonard's predicament, but none to his redemption. Leonard has no denouement. He has no beginning, no middle, no end. No satisfaction. No realization. No self-awareness. Yet Leonard is resolutely *selfish* in opposition to *other.*

And so we, too, are selfish during our experience of *Memento.* We have only what Leonard has: the immediacy of the moment, the engagement of desire, and a deeply imbedded—and flawed—sense of self. Like Leonard, we must both endure and deny the film's narrative. Our final pleasure in viewing *Memento* is not in finding a solution to its puzzles of logic, a solution that comes only belatedly, remains arbitrary, and resists scrutiny. The pleasures in *Memento* are in its denials, frustrations, and resonance with self.

If film is an illusion[27] of the sort Tan[28] and Anderson[29] speak, then *Memento* presents an illusion of an illusion. The movie finds its truth in self-reflections and re-representations, which become the only available path through an otherwise impenetrable labyrinth of false time, false play, and false narrative. In the revelation of truth through denial, the destructurings of play—in *Memento,* in the drama of Ionesco, in the fiction of Borges, in the compositions of Schonberg, in the fragile and fleeting art of the dadaists—accomplish aesthetically what the early Russian formalists referred to as *ostranenie.*[30]

Similarly, *Memento* defamiliarizes the movie experience through a recursive formal process: "film as illusion" as illusion. This same phenomenon of defamiliarization can be observed commonly and ubiquitously in many other characteristics of contemporary popular media. The car chase, the horror scene, the sexually explicit, the graphically obscene—each is an instance of some sudden and immediate spectacle[31] that does not advance or contribute to plot or narrative so much as each takes place outside those false structures in order to appeal more directly to an otherwise inarticulate self. The disjointed narratives of commercial television, the capsulated and repetitive formulas of pop music, and the mutable and expandable genres of advertisements, movie trailers, and machinima demand much more from and depend much more on viewer play—selfish play—than on designer structure.[32]

Digital games and related media refer us to experience through the physical distortions of joystick, thumb pad, keyboard, and mouse. This is not really running and jumping, *Mario's Adventures* shows us—yet it is. This is not really fear, *Silent Hill* shows us—yet it is. And this is not really narrative, *Memento* shows us—yet it is. And so, too, all running and jumping, all fear, and all narrative are not really such. The physical interface between our self and our world, so vital to the shared assumptions of conventional beliefs and values, is precisely the interface that digital media and play engage most actively and destroy most regularly.

An anti-aesthetic of play does not build human experience so much as it thwarts human experience and therein reveals otherwise hidden and binding processes guiding the building of human experience. Because of the peculiar nature of these processes and their intimate relation to self, it is impossible to reveal them through representational form alone. All structures, narratives, and languages—all representational forms—are false images of human experience and, therein, its antithesis. Play, on the other hand, is the embodiment of representational form and, therein, its revelation.

Often, the field of game studies attempts to contextualize play within games in order to serve the goals of game designers. But this contextualization assumes that play is capable of contextualization and that, within that contextualization, play is capable of direction, purpose, and design. The most basic aesthetic properties of play—its *pleasures*—seem counter to this assumption. If play is self-motivated, if it is *selfish*, then, regardless of designer intent, games and game studies of this narrative sort lie in dialectical opposition to the broader and proto-symbolic functions of human play.

CHAPTER 7

The Backstory

A masterpiece of fiction is an original world
and as such is not likely to fit the world of the reader.

—Vladimir Nabokov, *Lectures on Don Quixote* (1983)

Consider this rough model of the human meaning-making process (including generation of narrative):

- Sensory impressions engage mechanics of the human sensorium. These mechanics are determined by long-term evolutionary processes and, as such, are relatively intractable. This is the domain of *instinct.*
- Semiotic processes emerge through recursive and, possibly, unintended and unexpected uses of the mechanics of the sensorium. These uses, while they remain grounded in the neurophysiology of the sensorium, may exist in parallel—and, occasionally, in competition or even in conflict—with instinct. This is the domain of *play.*
- To the extent possible and beneficial, the outcomes—the values and meanings—of semiotic processes adapt and conform to sociological/cultural norms. This is the domain of *convention.*

THE BACKSTORY

The most obvious and common application of convention within computer games is the use of the ubiquitous "backstory." Conventionally, a backstory consists of "a narrative providing a history or background context, esp. for a character or situation in a literary work, film, or dramatic series."[1]

Backstories guide actors in creating characters in drama and guide writers in creating narratives in fiction. Soap operas, for instance, have extensive and complicated backstories used to justify character behavior. Computer game designers use backstories as design elements to achieve a consistent, coherent, and aesthetically pleasing implementation of game components. Ostensibly, backstories aid computer game players by delineating fundamental relationships among game objects and characters. Learning the backstory of the well-known and exemplary early adventure game *Myst* (1993), for instance, serves as both a source of clues to and the primary goal of game play.

There are two apparent reasons backstories have become common in the design and distribution of computer games. First, any series of human events—including play events—seems to motivate a natural semiotic contextualization process: a folk theory of causes. During extended play, player-characters are naturally conceived and valued as human-like entities acting according to a particular set of causes, that is, a narrative.

Second, game producers and designers are increasingly motivated—primarily for commercial reasons—to include backstories as a means of reproducing within alternative media the values and meanings that emerge during computer game play—through, for instance, "tie-ins." This is, of course, successful insofar as computer game backstories provide easily accessible examples of—and subsequently motivate—play. It is largely unsuccessful, however, wherever backstories are expected to determine, rather than exemplify, that play.

While narratives and backstories inevitably result from natural human semiosis, backstories neither motivate nor confine the semiotic process. Thus, backstories function very differently for computer game designers and for computer game players. For designers, backstories serve a framing function, making sure all game elements are implemented within a consistent, conventional, and (successfully) commercial context. For individual players, however, backstories inhibit the more *selfish* semiotic processes that occur during play.

This does not mean that backstories are not useful to and enjoyed by computer game players. Backstories obviously motivate individual and beginning play by exemplifying the (yet-to-be-experienced) outcomes of that play; and within some games—particularly within the genre of computer role-playing games—backstories may also contribute to an understanding of the context in which game elements are later most effectively manipulated and valued.

Most commonly and conventionally, however, backstories engage audiences simply by extending or expanding some previously experienced narrative. In extreme cases, this extension/expansion can blur the distinction between fiction and nonfiction—as in the detailed backstory accompanying the innovative release of *The Blair Witch Project* (1999), the conflation of fictional and real-life characters in the Web-based promotion of the HBO series *John from Cincinnati* (2007), and other similar viral marketing campaigns. In these cases and others, the narrative's backstory extends and broadens a preceding narrative form. This new and broader narrative context is then considered more informative and complete than the original.

By extending/expanding a narrative context in this way, backstories *recontextualize* narratives—that is, backstories transform the meanings of signs and symbols within a previous narrative by subsuming that narrative context within some other. Sometimes these transformations are mere confirmations of the meanings assigned by the original narrative, resulting in an *emphasis* of context; at other times, however, these transformations are more radical—as, for instance, when Tom Stoppard recontextualized *Hamlet* within *Rosencrantz and Guildenstern Are Dead* (1967)—resulting in the extension and expansion of context.

The semiotic function of backstories during computer game play might, then, be interpreted as either *convention* or *play*, depending on whether the previous narrative context is either emphasized or transformed. Most pertinent is the function of backstories during game design and during game play. Are these functions complementary? Do the conventions of designer-determined backstories aid or inhibit the novelties and transformations of individual play? Let me explore these questions as regards three popular and separate (though non-exclusive) genres of computer games: action, role-playing, and strategy games.

ACTION GAMES

In general, action games do not commonly use backstories, nor does their play particularly benefit from them. Young children's play and games—for example, peekaboo, chase, hide-and-seek—are of much the same semiotic class as computer action games. These children's games motivate the same fundamental semiotic processes as *Tetris*, the *Mario* game series, and virtually all first-person shooters (FPSs).

The signs and symbols of these games are interpreted without any immediate or necessary reference to narrative. Semiotic play in this genre involves the recognition of oppositional (most often visual) signs in a sensory context existing prior to either stories or storytelling. Of course, extended play of any sort eventually motivates some sort of contextualization process, and it is interesting to note how often this contextualization is accomplished within the action genre *without resort to conventional narrative form.* For instance, one of the most common methods of contextualization during action game play is to use an arbitrary context unconnected to the game play per se—that is, to attach to each episode of play a "score" that is then valued within the context of all scores of similar episodes of play. This linear sequence of scores—hopefully showing progression through "improvement"—then substitutes for narrative.

Another common technique of action game contextualization is to link isolated episodes of play within very generic contexts of human behavior—contexts so fundamental to the human experience that they avoid the narrative's conventional sequencing of events and any resulting values concerning cause, effect, or morality. For instance, the "backstory" in most FPSs can be reduced to a predator-prey relationship; if you understand this relationship (the basic relationship of "chase"), then you understand the context of FPS play more than well enough to play the FPS game, regardless of any broader narrative context within which that relationship might subsequently be placed.

> *DOOM* also had no real plot. Sure, it had a backstory to set the mood, but that's all it did. *DOOM* did not encumber you with annoying side characters or long, boring sections of Full Motion Video (like all those damned *Wing Commander* games, or *Jedi Knight* (ug, what a nightmare!)).[2]

More recently, a Tom Chick review of *Metal Gear 4*, decries how the backstory of the *Metal Gear* series has become so obtrusive that it interferes with the original goal and pleasures of FPS play.

> You're watching an indulgent series finale that exhaustively reiterates details and piles nonsensical twist on top of nonsensical twist. Without a degree in Metal Gear Solidology, you will be hopelessly lost, and by the time it's over, you will have long since ceased to care.[3]

Indeed, computer game players familiar with multiple genres of play immediately recognize the absence of backstory as an inconsequential element of play in arcade games, regardless of the length and complexity of that play. For instance, the *Mario* game series—produced/designed by Shigeru Miyamoto and originating with the arcade game *Donkey Kong* (1981)—has many superficial characteristics of role-playing games, but it remains rooted in the action genre due to, among other things, the inconsequential nature of its backstory.

None of the storylines answer some HUGE backstory questions, such as how the games tie together exactly, not to mention the relationship of the mushroom kingdom and other areas (Sarasaland anyone?) And what about the characters? What's their deeper motivation exactly? How old are they? What hand does Toad write with? And what about the koopa kids? Where'd they come from? And all these Yoshi's? How are they related? It's enough to make a guy go crazy![4]

Miyamoto's subsequent designs include the hugely successful *Zelda* games—beginning with *The Legend of Zelda* (1987)—each of which has increased the degree to which contextualization extends and expands game play. However, the *Zelda* series, despite an involved backstory involving Link and the Princess, remains very much action-oriented, and its design and play de-emphasize the importance of a backstory.

For every *Zelda* game we tell a new story . . . We actually have an enormous document that explains how the game relates to the others, and binds them together. But to be honest, they are not that important to us. We care more about developing the game system.[5]

ROLE-PLAYING GAMES

The genre of computer role-playing games (RPGs)—which includes computer adventure games as an intermediary form—is most fundamentally distinguished from the action genre by its reliance on the *expansion* of values and meanings during play. Whereas goals of action/arcade games[6] are determined by and accomplished with physical skills (and/or the hardware accoutrements) of game players, goals of adventure/role-playing games[7] are determined by and accomplished with more pragmatic and social skills of game players. Where action game goals are obvious but difficult to achieve, RPG goals are relatively more obscure but relatively easier to achieve. Consequently, single-player RPGs can and will be, inevitably, "won" by those who take the time to learn and play them thoroughly—not always the case with action games.

While the computer RPG genre makes much more frequent use of backstories than the action genre, it is interesting to note that the first design and publication of computer RPGs did not. Richard Garriott's *Akalabeth* (1980) was the progenitor of the long-running *Ultima* series and is arguably one of the more important prototypes for subsequent examples of the genre—including the many *Ultima* games, Sir-tech's *Wizardry* (1981), and, in a slightly later release, *Might and Magic* (1987). The original versions of these games had simple backstories that were superficial embellishments of generic themes, and game play in each tended to emphasize the action genre staple of monster bashing.

However, over time (and after the mechanics of RPGs had become entrenched), specialized backstories became an increasingly common—and much more detailed—design element.

> *Might and Magic I* came with a forty-page manual. The first quarter of this manual described how to create characters prior to play, the rest concerned the mechanics of play . . . The first game manual did not refer to narrative structures . . . unique to the *M&M* game world . . . The manual of the next *Might and Magic* game (*II: Gates to Another World*) devoted its first 2500 words to a history of the expanding *M&M* game context. And each manual thereafter added . . . further information about preexisting characters and legends within the *M&M* fantasy universe.[8]

Let me use the extended example of *Ultima* and its related online descendant, *Ultima Online* (*UO*), as an example of the characteristic elements of computer RPGs and the function (or dysfunction) of backstories within them.

Ultima has one of the longer histories in the design and evolution of computer RPGs. The *Ultima* series began with the rudimentary *Akalabeth,* a fairly simple dungeon crawl inspired by, as most early computer RPGs were, the paper-and-pencil game *Dungeons & Dragons*—which, in turn, owes much to the rules of miniature wargames (e.g., *Chainmail*) and the novels of Jack Vance. To the extent that computer RPGs are based on such preexisting sets of character relationships, scenarios, and goals, all computer RPGs can be said to have a similar generic backstory (e.g., the heroic quest).

The common backstory guiding the original *Ultima* games was not unique and required no advanced training or knowledge prior to play. Richard Garriott was, in fact, "particularly pleased" that playing the first *Ultima* games required "no main menu, no outside the game activity of any kind." "You could install it," he said, "and then, suddenly, go directly into game play."[9]

Garriott became concerned, however, that generic adaptations of the *Dungeons & Dragons* system promoted a hack-and-slash, pillage-and-plunder style of play, which was, in his mind, more synonymous with villainy than heroism. By *Ultima IV* (1985), Garriott's game designs purposefully emphasized the ethical consequences of character behavior and displayed what would come to be known as the *Ultima* "virtue system." Design elements such as the *Ultima* virtue system—along with recurring characters and a consistent game world—greatly aided the natural development of narrative within the *Ultima* game series. That is, knowledge of these elements provided insight into the proper interpretation of game signs and symbols through an ongoing narrative associated with the hero (Avatar) player-character; therefore, it was beneficial to play the *Ultima* games, like a narrative, in the sequence they were written, published, and distributed. Or, at least, this was intent of the game designer.

> The real advantage of playing the previous ones is that you kind of *get* it . . . There's a lot of history to really understand the virtues and its meaningful backbone to the story . . . and I think you'll find it much more meaningful.[10]

However, those design elements functioning as backstory were more often interpreted by game players as just another part of the game rules—not especially significant. That is, playing the *Ultima* game series by adhering strictly to the moral code of a "good-guy" Avatar—as valued by the game's backstory and as intended by the game designer—was neither the quickest nor, for many, the most fun way to play the game. More often, the early, single-player *Ultima* games were played, by designers and players alike,[11] in an "achiever" style of play that de-prioritized the game's backstory and, in some cases, ignored it entirely.

> Achievers regard points-gathering and rising in levels as their main goal, and all is ultimately subservient to this.[12]

Realizing this, Richard Garriott more purposively incorporated *Ultima's* backstory into the rules of the single-player game series and assessed player penalties for "unethical" behavior within the game. However, these player penalties likewise came to be valued solely within the context of the game rules—and therein isolated from the more conventional and restrictive functions of the game's backstory. This resulted in players seeking active means to transform and avoid the penalties associated with player-character unethical behavior (totally OK within the context of the game *code*) rather than seeking to avoid unethical behavior itself (more appropriate within the context of the game *narrative*).

In this way, the transformations of play "trumped" the narrative conventions of the backstory (rather than vice versa). This remained equally true of *Ultima*'s successor, *Ultima Online.*

The designers of *UO* (Garriott was, by this time, removed from the project) also went to great lengths to promote appropriate game values (e.g., no player killing) by providing voluminous backstories justifying and exemplifying the *Ultima* virtue system.[13] Many design changes implemented since the online game's initial release[14] likewise attempted to make the *Ultima* virtue system and its related backstory more integral to game play. However, the largest portion of the *UO* player population continued to play the game with no reference to or comment on the designer-generated backstory. Indeed, game play in *Ultima Online* seemed as often motivated by factors outside the game entirely (e.g., the economic system of eBay) than by a predetermined, in-game narrative.

Herein lies a thorny issue regarding the use of backstories in the design of RPGs. Backstories appear to motivate game players to buy (or simply play) a game. And game play appears to motivate values and meanings that are then naturally incorporated into stories, narratives, and, if available and possible, backstories. Indeed, my own observations of early computer role-playing games and gamers[15] found many instances in which narratives of all sorts were used to value game symbols and outcomes. However, these narratives were always constructed *by players as a result of play.* Only as an afterthought did these narratives conform to backstories constructed by game designers prior to individual play.

Most often, play within the role-playing genre remains, like play within the action game genre, a meaning-*making* process—not a process of meaning confirmation or meaning validation. This makes it very difficult for any single and self-consistent backstory to contain the great barrage of meanings generated during play.

Even so-called master or grand backstories[16] provide little "story" other than the generic predator-prey relationship so common in the action game genre. Any further, more detailed explication of character relationships— that is, explication leading to a more robust folk theory of causes, like that of the *UO* virtue system—is eventually rendered superfluous during extended play. Extended play in RPGs—for both designers and players—is almost always devoted to issues of play *balance* rather than play *narrative.* Indeed, insofar as narratives privilege one sort of character or one sort of meaning over some other, narratives pose a semiotic context antithetical to games and play—despite the often finely detailed backstories game designers devote so much time and effort to create.[17]

While backstories do not carry great weight for experienced and expert game players, RPG backstories do seem to engage a particular sort of player who is primarily interested in the peripheries of computer game play: the "fanboy." The fanboy—usually a pejorative term, meant to include both males and females—is a relatively new phenomenon within computer gaming. In my early observations of computer games and gamers, I found little reference to fanboy types, whereas this segment of the computer gaming population is currently difficult to miss. Fanboys are similar in many respects to Bartle's socializer type[18] but do most (if not all) of their socializing *outside the context of the game rules.* In fact, long-lived games in which rules become well-known and widely distributed—such as *Ultima* and *Ultima Online* and other games with multi-year histories—seem to have relatively fewer fanboys than newer, less thoroughly learned and tested games. This may be because fanboys are more attracted to genre than game and, correspondingly, more attracted to narrative than play. The beta versions of many online games, for instance, are often frequented by fanboys without regard to the mechanics or balance of game play (since those are, within the beta category, still undetermined).

With little regard for the details of game rules, fanboys can be observed across all genres of games. There are fanboys within the action game genre whose devotion is as often to a particular game platform as to a particular game. And there are fanboys within the strategy game genre, as well, in which detailed backstories can more actively interfere with game play.

STRATEGY GAMES

Early and prototypical examples of computer strategy games include *Hammurabi, Civilization, SimCity, Master of Orion,* and many other games in which game rules and game play transform, to a greater or lesser extent, the game rules. This transformation process is simultaneously critical to the strategy genre and contrary to the function of narrative as a theory of causes. Again, close examination of a single example is informative. Let me use the *Master of Orion* series as an example of the difficulties involved in attempting to frame strategy game play within the values of a backstory.

Master of Orion (*MOO*), published in 1993, was a fairly typical (now classic) game with 4X strategy (explore, expand, exploit, exterminate).[19] It was released with a minimal backstory. Players could choose to be one of several intergalactic species (the Alkari, fast but weak bird-like creatures; the Bulrathi, slow but strong bearlike creatures; etc.) in competition over some limited number of star systems.

Thrown into this zoological mix were the remnants of a technologically superior uber-race, the Orions, who were eventually replaced by the player winning the game. There was a bit more about the origin of the mysterious Orions and such, but none of the game's early backstory had any real impact on game play. *MOO* play consisted of, as all strategy game play does, valuing the advantages and disadvantages of one species, weapon, and/or tactic against the advantages and disadvantages of some other. Most important, this balancing act of determining the relative value of game objects could be done most thoroughly and accurately with no reference to the game's backstory whatsoever.

During play, in fact, the *MOO* backstory became increasingly superfluous. The competition among the intergalactic species within the game could have easily taken place within a fantasy world or an ancient civilization or beneath the surface of an isolated pond of scum. What mattered was not the setting or the characters or the plot but the *relationships* among the game's signs and symbols as adjudicated by the game rules—and, of course, how these relationships were transformed (i.e., valued in real-time) during play.

The original *MOO* was popular enough to generate a sequel, *Master of Orion II: Battle at Antares* (*MOO2*), in 1996. And just as in the case of the *Ultima* game series, the extension of play from *MOO* to *MOO2* generated a more detailed backstory. In *MOO2*, the Orions were supplemented by the evil Antarans, another technologically advanced race, which was eventually replaced by the player winning the game. While the core game mechanics remained the same, a variety of embellishments extended play within the familiar context of the original game. And while the *MOO2* backstory implied a meaningful connection between the two games, neither game required knowledge of the other to play. Both games were independently and widely praised.

In 2003 came *Master of Orion III* (*MOO3*), which was considered both by reviewers and by players to be broken. Why was *MOO3* such a dismal failure, while *MOO* and *MOO2* were such major successes? At least part of the reason can be attributed to the emphasis given to the *MOO3* backstory during the game's design. It is difficult to trace in detail the *MOO3* design process because that process took so long (over three years) and involved so many different designers—including several who were subsequently removed from the project. Alan Emrich,[20] one of those removed, had this to say early about the emphasis on narrative within *MOO3*:

I believe in stories so much that I want players to get output at the end of the game . . . It will keep track of everything they do. Every leader who was raised and lost, every battle, every policy, everything. This huge text file is the chronicle of your civilization. And you can take that and literally write your own story from that outline.[21]

This goal is not inconsistent with a common result of strategy game play and, in fact, play in general. Players commonly work singly or in groups, rightly or wrongly, with some effort, to shape a theory of causes—a narrative—explaining and justifying game outcomes. Given this tendency, any game design aiding the post-play, meaning-structuring process (e.g., as the *Civilization* series did with its saved game timelines) is welcome.

However, later *MOO3* design efforts, headed most visibly by Rantz Hosely (art director) and Cory Nelson (producer) at Quicksilver Software, emphasized how narratives were to be used to tie together the three *MOO* games and, simultaneously, provide a context of design for future games. This emphasis is made clear within a variety of *MOO3* pre-release interviews given by the Quicksilver design team.

> We went over the basis/setting for *Star Lords* (pre-*MOO1*), *MOO1,* and *MOO2.* These became the keystones for the history arc . . . *Master of Orion,* with two previous incarnations, already had elements established . . . but no overarching story or background that tied it all together. In talking with Microprose at the time, we were given the license and encouraged to flesh the *Master of Orion* universe out, with an eye not only on what the current project was, but also looking at the possibility of sequels, prequels, [in order to] establish a firm base to support the franchise for future projects . . . (A *MOO* RPG for example.)[22]

During the period prior to the release of *MOO3,* the game's backstory was a source of great interest (and play) for many within online forums devoted to the discussion of the *Master of Orion* series, such as the Infogrames (subsequently Atari) forums and the Apolyton Web site.[23] And prior to the release of the game, the game's backstory received a favorable response from fanboys and strategy game aficionados alike. After the game's release however, these two groups were polarized; fanboys continued to champion the game's backstory, while strategy game players much more negatively evaluated *MOO3* game elements based on game play. In fact, the pre-release interest devoted to *MOO3* character backgrounds, appearances, and dramatic roles within the game's backstory became a source of irritation for many players.

The really disappointing part is that the initial *Master of Orion* got the aliens right. Sure, they were goofy, but . . . for the purposes of playing a game, that works out wonderfully. These guys [the *MOO3* design team] just had trouble determining what was important and what was trivial.[24]

Yet another article about the "details of their space strategy game" that manages to not put in a single comment about the things that matter . . . It ain't art. It ain't animations. It ain't whether or not there's a backstory, if there are diplomatic animations, or anything else involving writing a story (i.e. authoring) or producing an image or animation of some type (i.e. artistry of many types and sorts).[25]

In this regard—in their inability to benefit from detailed narratives during play—interactive computer games appear a relatively unique form of popular entertainment. Unlike the common experiences associated with non-computer-based entertainment—*Harry Potter* novels, *X-men* comic books, anime of various sorts—computer game play is more often severely and adversely affected by a predetermined narrative frame. Or, put more generally perhaps, human play necessarily exists outside a theory of causes.

The inability of computer game backstories to function in a consistent manner, with the same degree of success, as backstories in other aesthetic forms indicates that computer games are fundamentally different from those other forms. While semiotic values and outcomes emerging from computer game play are commonly combined into narratives, those narratives are an imposition on the values and outcomes—the transformations—of play. That is, the production of values and outcomes during play is neither caused nor determined by backstories.

In this sense, human play can be considered a *pre-narrative* act, existing outside a theory of causes. In fact, in order to generate true novelty, play *must* exist outside all conventional theories of causes: play must be paradoxical. For this reason, no doubt, play continues to appear instinctive, intractable, and, to some degree, unpredictable. Each of these characteristics is then also a fundamental characteristic of human semiosis, which remains closely intertwined with the nature and function of play.

In order to examine this relationship between human play and human semiosis in greater detail, let me consider further one of the most popular, sophisticated, and exemplary forms in the evolution of the computer strategy game genre: the *Civilization* game series.

CHAPTER 8

Civilization

> All of my games are based on stuff I was interested in at the time.
> —Sid Meier, Gamespy (2005)

I first found myself writing about *Sid Meier's Civilization*—using it, along with Mark Baldwin's *Empire* (Interstel, 1987), as a prototypical example of computer strategy games—shortly after the game's commercial release by Microprose just before Christmas 1991.[1]

In the succeeding decade, the game has seen several major revisions (*Civilization II,* Microprose, 1996; *Civilization III,* Infogrames, 2001; *Civilization IV,* 2K Games, 2005), numerous supplements, mods, copycat designs, and, in the wake of widespread play and commercial success, a great variety of reviews, commentaries, and scholarly analyses. Over this period, my interest in the game—as a player and a critic—has seldom waned (though, admittedly, *Civilization III* tested that interest a bit). In *The Nature of Computer Games,* I devoted a chapter to the evolution of the *Civilization* game series, emphasizing components of *Civ* play that reflect recursive and transformative properties of cognitive play with computer games.

Currently, the *Sid Meier's Civilization* series remains one of the most interesting—and most fun—instances of a "builder," a computer strategy game in which player goals fall into the well-known 4X categories: explore, expand, exploit, exterminate. But perhaps even more intriguing is that *Civ* has become, in the brief history of computer gaming, a *mature* game—that is, an illuminating example of how computer games are shaped and refined over time in response to the gathered experiences of their players. It is this maturity of *Civilization* play that I wish to emphasize here: namely, the game's seemingly limitless *replayability* and the manner in which that replayability is critical to an understanding of cognitive play.

SAVING, RELOADING, AND REPLAY

Replay is an integral component of the play process and, as such, is not restricted to play with computer games. However, play with computer games displays informative manifestations of game replay—for example, *save-and-reload* play.

All computer game players are familiar with save-and-reload strategies, which are applied within a great variety of games. In brief, saving and reloading involves initially playing some portion of a game (perhaps even its entirety), often less than satisfactorily; this portion of the game is then replayed, with some portion of that replay duplicative of the play preceding it. Common examples are found in first-person shooters in which the player-character dies in confrontation with a powerful opponent; the game player must then reload (or reboot) in order to face the same opponent again. This replay process gives computer game play a *spiral-like* (as opposed to a linear) trajectory.[2]

Very similar replay occurs in action games, in role-playing games, and in computer strategy games such as *Civilization*. And while there are subtle differences in the function of saving and reloading among computer game genres—at least partly justifying and verifying genre classification systems—the fundamental nature and basic characteristics of replay are common. Indeed, in many cases where the "saving" component of saving-and-reloading is either omitted or prohibited by game design, "reloading" and replay occur nevertheless. For instance, unlike home computer games, arcade computer games traditionally provide players no opportunity to save game positions and continue play at a later date. Yet arcade games derive their popularity—and their income—precisely from extensive replay.

Replay is common not only across computer game genres but also across computer game histories—particularly within game histories as relatively long and detailed as that of *Civilization*. Replay in *Civilization* occurs both within the computer game proper and also within the extended process of play that has resulted in *Civilization*'s various versions, revisions, and alternate designs. Incorporating ubiquitous replay, the "spiral-like" trajectory of computer game play is more accurately *recursive*, wherein replay is both persistent, iterative and, most significantly, transformative.

Though I have already elsewhere detailed a history of *Civilization* design,[3] let me briefly recount and update the pertinent aspects of that history here.

The first *Civilization* computer game—designed in tandem by Sid Meier and Bruce Shelley in 1991—originated as a redesign (or replay) of Frances Tresham's earlier board game (Hartland Trefoil, 1980). Ostensibly a simulation of the growth of ancient civilizations within the Mediterranean oval, the board game's most unique and compelling feature was its use of civilization "advances" that transformed game play at various points during play. That is, these advances transformed the relative value of game units in such a way that game players were forced to revalue and redo their play (i.e., to replay). After a civilization advance had appeared, a pacifist player might be forced to adopt a more aggressive position; or an expansionist player might be forced to devote more time and attention to local city maintenance; or, more radically, a player with a previously unassailable position might realize that her newly transformed position was suddenly hopeless and might be forced to start the game anew.

The Meier/Shelley design made much of these civilization "advances," turning them into the computer game's "World Wonders"—for example, the Pyramids and the Sistine Chapel. World Wonders were such an important part of *Civilization* play that expert and winning play was determined almost solely by predicting and controlling when and under whose ownership the World Wonders appeared.

While other design elements and rules of the first *Civilization* computer game also involved contextual transformations—for example, the tilling of virtual landscape by workers and the celebratory benefits of an array of city improvements—the peculiar transformations wrought by the World Wonders were neither so localized nor so limited. Indeed, the World Wonder transformations were, in an important way, transformations of the game itself; as a result, it was practically impossible to learn the rules of the game until you had played—and replayed—those portions of the game in which those rules were transformed. For this reason, replay within *Civilization* became, over time, increasingly analytical and abstract, as the (re) player came to be guided by goals and strategies determined by *meta*-rules (e.g., rules for the transformation of rules) that were unavailable for novice players.

It is also interesting to note[4] that this repetitive, recursive aspect of *Civilization* game play was mirrored by (and perhaps even resulted from) the repetitive, recursive process of its design. During the design of the original *Civilization*, Shelley tended to be the game player, and Meier tended to be the game coder. Over the course of approximately a year prior to the release of *Sid Meier's Civilization*, Meier continuously varied the game code (transforming the rules governing game play), and Shelley continuously valued the game play (determining, according to meta-rules of play, which game rules should and would be further transformed in subsequent variations).

Through a similar but vastly extended process of play and replay, wherein the first release of the game was played, replayed, and valued within a growing community of players, *Civilization* spawned *Civilization II* and *Civilization III* and, later, after a complex series of sales and transfers of publishing rights, *Civilization IV*. These later games—most particularly *Civilization II*—were each blatant redesigns of their predecessor(s). These redesigns attempted both to eliminate "bad" game elements and to expand and refine "good" game elements. And what's most important is the degree to which "good" and "bad" were definitively determined only through the extended process of play and replay.

> So we got our fun experts together and began the mammoth task of sorting through ideas . . . In the years since *Civilization* first appeared we have received literally thousands of letters, phone calls, and e-mail messages offering suggestion for improvements, additions, and sequels . . .
>
> Of course, the biggest potential pitfall in working on a game like this is that none of us wanted to go down in history as "they guys who broke *Civilization*"! . . . Every addition or change needed to be carefully weighted to make sure it wasn't doing more harm than good.[5]

Game design elements common among (and thus proved by the test of replay within) all games in the *Civilization* series included such crucial components as the transformation capabilities of the World Wonders, the basic goals of the 4X genre, and the game's (at least superficial) resemblance to the cultural history and characteristics of real-world civilizations. Game design elements unique to the first *Civilization* (and thus at some point revised/ removed during the redesign process) included the original game's visual appearance, its operating system, and the various rules that came to be associated with unsatisfactory—broken—play.

"Broken" rules in *Civilization* included—and, in fact, were characterized by—rules that allowed the game to be won by avoiding the transformations of replay. During broken play, the spiral-like progression of *Civilization* play—as envisioned by the game's designers and enjoyed by its players—was short-circuited. Commonly, this resulted from some imbalance within the rules, favoring one portion of those rules (or rules-based strategies) over others; this imbalance drastically curtailed replay in that the game context then remained static—untransformed—from one game or session of game play to the next. That is, the game could be won—and won very quickly—in a manner that made the full range of World Wonder transformations largely irrelevant and, in some cases, entirely superfluous. If so, then over time and replay, the game became increasingly less fun.

> The Parallelia and Mongol strategies are game-beating strategies that exploit loopholes in versions 1.0 and 2.0 of *Civilization.* Both of them are fairly sure wins at any difficulty level, but they remove much of the enjoyment of playing *Civilization.*[6]

The challenge facing successive redesigns of any popular game, such as *Civilization,* is to add complexity and value without destroying the original game's appeal. The successful redesign of *Civilization* within each subsequent edition exemplifies the degree to which recursive replay was fundamental to the original *Civilization*'s popularity. Throughout the *Civilization* series of games, learning the game rules remained a recursive process that, even once that process was well understood and widely practiced by the game's most dedicated players, preceded in a recursive fashion *without any certainty of a definitive outcome.*

> The spiral does not end because it cannot end—not without destroying the playing. Play is, in fact, never a spiral, always a spiraling.[7]

A THEORETICAL INTERLUDE

Recursive replay, as observed within the behavior of computer game designers and players, is often referred to obliquely by game theorists and critics as either an inclusive process motivated by the peculiar characteristics of digital media (e.g., Bolter's and Grusin's *remediation*) or a more exclusive process narrowly focused on those stories, narratives, and other literary devices that are assumed to mediate computer game play.[8] Here, however, recursive replay is more properly associated with basic human neurophysiology and universal cognitive practice, regardless of either the context in which that process operates (e.g., new media) or the objects on which that process operates (e.g., either "ergodic" texts or narratives). Assuming a natural-historical origin of play as a biological imperative, this process stands alone.[9]

Many analyses of computer games disagree. For instance, among technology-based theorists—including (with a broad brush) Manovich (2002) and Kittler (1997)—recursion and its manifestation as replay within computer games are shaped by and understood only with reference to some preexisting social, cultural, and/or related technological context.

Similarly, text-based theories—including those advanced by Aarseth (1997), Ryan (1992), and much of the hypertext/interactive-fiction group (see, e.g., Montfort 2003)—most comfortably attach recursion and replay to a particular type of sign and symbol system, whether this system is as vague as language or as limited as narrative.

Both these two theoretical positions—the tech-based and the text-based—seem to assume that the "meaning" of play and replay is largely predetermined by the unique constraints (or, sometimes, freedoms) that digital media and/or digital texts impose on computer game players and play or, alternatively, that this "meaning" is determined on the fly, as a consequence of the immersion of game play and players within the contingencies of an immediate and ongoing process of social and cultural negotiation regarding individual values and meanings.

In contrast, if recursive replay is indeed integral to the hard-wired mechanics of a biologically determined play, and if play is indeed integral to human cognition, then computer game play need not be constrained (or explained) by external factors. The constraints of play—insofar as those constraints would be knowable through cognition—would be wholly determined by the boundaries of cognition. That is, play might well appear paradoxical (i.e., characterized by epistemic conflicts on the boundaries of the knowable); it might also appear instinctive (i.e., without any directly knowable cause). Play would, in such a scenario, appear to simply bootstrap itself into existence, either in ignorance or blatant disregard of rules or expectations contrary to its most fundamental form.

Recursive replay within *Civilization*—and, in fact, replay within all computer games—displays many of these characteristics of paradox and self-determination. For instance, while computer games normally have clearly defined goals (the *Civilization* series has always had multiple winning conditions: military victory, cultural domination, winning the race to Alpha Centauri, etc.), the process necessary to achieve those goals involves transforming the game context in a manner that quite clearly moves those goals further away: the proverbial carrot on a stick. Players engage in such a paradoxical, recursive process instinctively during replay, often without full realization of its implications. Game designers implement a cascading series of recursive goals more consciously and purposefully—most obviously as a series of difficulty levels that eventually recede beyond human capabilities.

> It was also clear that the forty bazillion or so hours of playing time which have occurred between 1991 and the present have served to vastly improve the world's overall *Civ*-playing skills . . . Without making the game more difficult for beginners, we needed to crank up the challenge level significantly for all the jaded experts out there. . . . Finally, we added the new Deity difficulty level for those who like their *Civ* really mean.[10]

Certainly, over time, the *Civilization* redesigns have increased the number of player options—and related player challenges—far beyond the probability that any single player, during any single lifetime, will exhaustively complete them all. The appeal of such a multiplicity of game-related tasks (short of playing the game in its entirety) must then be found in the game's *perceived* completability, regardless of how many goals or tasks are actually completed at the end of some interminable series of plays and replays. In such a context, the pleasures of play appear to result from two simultaneous and seemingly contradictory desires: first, the desire to conceive a clear end to play (e.g., in terms of designer-imposed goals); and second, a persistent unwillingness to reach that end. Only the first of these two might be significantly affected by game design; and, in fact, when confronted with designer-imposed goals that prove less than satisfactory—that is, game goals too easily or too quickly achieved—recursive replay bootstraps itself: players impose their own indeterminable goals, such as the herculean One-City Challenge[11] in *Civilization II*.

The embedded "challenge" of a game is thus far less important than the player's perception of the challenging; and this perception is, then, less clearly motivated by any objective characteristic(s) of game design than by those phenomenological, self-determined processes embedded in ongoing cognitive play. Successful game rules do not *construct* play; successful game rules *conform* to a preexisting set of natural-historical rules governing cognitive play.

I pause to make this point clearly regarding play and replay within *Civilization* because implications and predictions are quite distinct among tech-based and text-based approaches and my own "brain-based" approach—as I have distinguished those three here—to the study of computer game play.

Most particularly, there are significant differences in the predictions these make concerning the *effects* of games and game play.

The *Civilization* series has the superficial trappings of a historical simulation. Indeed, some of the scenarios built into the game allow players to play on a realistically drawn (to some rough level of approximation) map of Earth; the names of the civilizations included in the game are the names of real-life nations and peoples; and the city improvements, unit types, and political systems referred to in the game are all represented at some basic, though often abstract, level of verisimilitude. In general, then, the signs and symbols of the *Civilization* series are similar to those signs and symbols found in more conventional accounts of human civilization and progress, such as history texts.

Further, many have found parallels between the "lessons" learned or the "stories" told during *Civilization* game play and various political ideologies and/or broad-based assumptions about the nature of Earth's peoples and their relationships. These lessons/stories have been, on different occasions, interpreted both positively[12] and negatively.[13] However, regardless of any normative issues involved, these lessons/stories are assumed to be embedded in the game design and, subsequently, within the play that the design motivates. Based on how *Civilization* is actually played and replayed, I would like to use the remainder of this chapter to debunk this notion.

PLAY AND REPLAY—WITH MEANING THIS TIME

Cognitive play within the *Civilization* series is only marginally different from play within many other, similar computer games—most particularly those games within the 4X, builder genre. Cognitive play evokes a play and replay process that transforms signs and symbols just as often and just as radically as the World Wonders transform the game context within *Civilization*. This results in game signs and symbols having significantly different meanings than those meanings to which they are conventionally assigned outside the context of play.

Indiscriminate Bombings

The initial release of *Civilization* generated a (sometimes quite heated) controversy concerning the game's implementation of nuclear power.

There are several victory conditions available within the *Civilization* games—some variable and chosen by the player before the game begins. Traditional and commonplace ways to win the game include (the typical wargame fare of) destroying all your opponents and, a bit more imaginatively, winning a space race to Alpha Centauri. The condition of victory in the space race can be chosen to guide play from the beginning of the game, or it can be selected as a fall-back position to be used any time a military victory proves unlikely. Computer-run civilizations, in fact, if sensing military defeat, devote their resources to the option of the space race—forcing the hand of opposing military commanders by changing the pace at which attacking forces must be mustered and deployed.

Such a sudden transformation of game context and goals—and related game rules—is a dedicated feature of the World Wonders, which, in the endgame, include the chief determinant of the space race: the Apollo Project. Also included in the *Civilization* endgame, for much the same reason—to move the game's goals a little further from the player's event horizon—are industrial pollution and, most particularly, pollution associated with nuclear power, plants, and bombs.

In the typical *Civilization* endgame, with over-large cities strewn across a modernist landscape, pollution and accompanying global warming become a major problem. In fact, the steadily increasing pollution rates—along with the late-game World Wonders—mark the final transformation of the game's early and mid-game goals to the endgame goals of either city destruction (the military version) or city exodus (the version of the space race).

Some have interpreted the implementation of nuclear power within the game and the resulting, inevitable decay of the *Civilization* landscape as carrying political connotations *beyond the context of the game*. The argument goes something like this:

> Players must . . . take care to preserve the environment. Too many large, polluting cities, for example, can lead to ecological disasters, ranging from the destruction of local environments to global warming. Pollution also affects the players' final score: players lose "civilization points" for every square of polluted terrain. Such features have led some to conclude that the game has an environmental message. Others have criticized the game for its cultural bias. Justin Hall, for example, remarks that the game reflects the "high technology late capitalist mindset of America."[14]

From the beginning, Sid Meier has consistently denied any intention of using the *Civilization* game designs as political statements, as indicated in this remark from a *CGOnline* interview:

> It's a gameplay factor. We very consciously avoid putting our political philoso-

phy into the game. . . . Now, it did seem, and I think it turned out to be true, that building that element into Civilization, the pollution and things like that, gave you a new challenge as you got to the later parts of the game . . . So pollution became that kind of thing.[15]

Given the common and characteristically incomplete nature of replay, it is problematic what portion of *Civilization* players (and critics) have gained full access to the later stages of the game and experienced the effects of pollution *in a recursive context of play*. Many obviously have and do, though it is also reasonable to assume that more players reach the final stages of the game (*any* game) on lower difficulty levels than they do on the highest possible difficulty level.

In any case, it is only during initial and novice play—which is most compatible with a linear reading of game as text—that *Civilization* game signs and symbols (i.e., game *signifiers*) might be reasonably associated with those preexisting—often normative—values corresponding to the use (or misuse) of real-world factories, fossil fuels, and nuclear energies (i.e., real-world *signifieds*). During and after repeated play of *Civilization,* there are at least two factors that make this tentative association between game signifiers and real-world signifieds unlikely.

First, and most specifically as regards the *Civilization* series, the games are neither historical simulations nor historical texts, despite that fact that they are sometimes referred to as such—in both scholarly and popular publications.[16] Technical reasons for this are embedded in the game's semiotic structure,[17] but let me simply note again that *Civilization* has been designed and redesigned—beginning with the original Meier and Shelley efforts—to quite clearly conform to an aesthetics of play rather than to construct a realistic model of human history. And over the succeeding years, the games have retained the trappings of a historical simulation only in the most superficial and nominative sense.[18]

Second, and more important as regards computer game play in general, interactive game *play*—not game readings and not isolated game components and structures—most definitively maps, measures, and gives meaning to the signs and symbols within a game. The best test of this claim lies in the experiences of—and the choices made by—game players. Do these choices in any way reflect those cultural values commonly attributed to game components—for example, the nuclear-power complex of signs—*outside the context of play*?

As an example of how and why *Civilization* players come to value game elements, consider again the alternative (and aberrant) strategies available to players of the original *Civilization*—the same version wherein the controversy concerning the use of nuclear power originated. One of the most aberrant of these strategies was the so-called Mongol strategy, a version of the well-known "rush" (or "zerg") technique, which is often used as a first test of game balance and artificial intelligence capabilities by players of turn-based and, in particular, real-time computer strategy games (e.g., the *Age of Empires* series).

The "value" of a Mongol strategy in *Civilization*—positive in terms of winning the game; negative in terms of curtailing replay (and fun)—was determined solely by its effect on the individual play experience. Certainly, the game rules allowing successful use of the Mongol strategy were not seen—by either players or critics of the game—as an editorial comment concerning the relative superiority of the Mongol civilization. These rules were simply ultimately and inevitably not fun, so these rules were ultimately and inevitably revised in subsequent game designs, *regardless of their value or meaning outside the context of play*. At the same time, complaints about the implementation of nuclear power within *Civilization* have seldom referenced any negative impact on the immediate play experience, so the function of nuclear power within the game has been changed very little in the game's many revisions.

In general, sociocultural critics of *Civilization*'s ideological biases have not found it necessary to look at specific strategies employed by expert players prior to assuming widespread effects of those biases. Yet the most frequently discussed aspects of the game within dedicated player forums (e.g., on the Apolyton Web site) are the relationships among in-game signifieds—without reference to or really any concern about their significance (or signification) outside the game context. As a result, these discussions of game rules and related strategies have greater relevance to other computer strategy games than they do to the real-world referents of the game's signs and symbols. This is true both of the topics of player-based game analyses and of the methods employed by those analyses—both are quite different from the topics and methods employed by sociocultural theorists.

Here, for instance, is a typical gamer's approach to valuing rush strategies as they (re-)appear within the single and multiplayer versions of *Civilization III*. (In this particular context, the aberrant Mongol strategy has evolved into a more efficient, virus-like form: the "Infinite City Strategy," or ICS.)

> Enter the first release of CivIII with its flog hack of pop-rushing, and for a while ICS was back with a vengence. Everything the Civ team had done to

butt °°°° big city strategies, and there is no other term for it—such as resource problems, worse corruption, harder unhappiness, more aggressive AI
civs, less effective research for players than for AIs—made ICS ever more
attractive . . .

The recent patch is like a late Beta of a working game, the first release was
like an Alpha. ICS is a good ma[r]ker of how well play tested a civ version
was. It is an obvious, easy strategy, like "imp" from corewars, that crushes
more elegant and complex strategies. If it works too well, then the version
hasn't been well thought out.[19]

This particular player analysis—representative of many others—assigns
value to new game elements (e.g., "pop-rushing") within the context of the
entire set of *Civilization* game rules (i.e., in relationship to rules determining
"resource problems, worse corruption, harder unhappiness, more aggressive
AI civs," etc.). This assignation occurs without reference to either the historical accuracy or the real-world value of game elements. And, importantly, this
assignation occurs only as a result of knowledge gained through extensive
replay.

If there is any most obvious bias in player analysis of this sort, it is the bias
of the engineer in adopting a systems approach to determining values for
game units. However, any such bias in methodology does not undermine the
overwhelming tendency of game players to adjudicate game units, designs,
rules, and related strategies according to their impact on *subjective* game
experiences (or according to what I referred to earlier as an "aesthetic of
play"), as in the reference in the preceding quote to "elegant and complex"
strategies.

Barbarous Treatments

The *Civilization* "barbarian" game element—appearing in the earliest portions of all games in the *Civilization* series—has received critical attention
similar to that of pollution in the late game. Barbarian interpretations and values differ sharply in the analysis of game players and of sociocultural critics.

In those analyses valuing *Civilization* game signs as at least some part of
a colonialist/imperialist manifesto (see the quotes that follow), the treatment
of barbarians as distinct from the more cultured, scientifically endowed, and
eventually successful player civilizations forces game-world barbarians into
a subordinate relationship with the player civilizations, a relationship that
reflects similar treatments imposed and assumptions held outside the game
context.

The equation that the player has to make between the Barbarian's level of nomadic activity and [the] threat they pose, points to a western [sic] mentality in which nomadic behavior is placed on the periphery of the culture as the "other."[20]

The Indians exist not as a civilization in their own right, but as an obstacle to be surmounted by civilization; in the [*Civilization*] game, as in Rowlandson's account, the enemy Indian Other is imagined as being the mechanism whereby the nascent American self is tested and found to be powerful.[21]

There is no doubt that recursive play as I have described it—reflecting basic patterns of human cognition—is universally involved in categorizing and, indeed, evoking oppositional relationships between self and other. However, there remains little evidence that the objects valued within such an opposition (i.e., signifiers of "other") carry the same meanings or significations inside the game as they do outside the game. In fact, there are contrary indications.

For instance, Douglas (2002) acknowledges that most players come to designate the barbarian villages as "goody huts," a label more clearly reflecting their role in the game than their ideological value to invading Western civilizations. From a gamer's point of view, in fact, the role of barbarians during play is more help than hindrance.

The most obvious function of the barbarians in the original *Civilization* design was to contribute to the game's variable difficulty levels. However, the impact of barbarians on game play is actually quite small, particularly when the game's difficulty level is set on anything other than its lowest levels. Barbarians indeed pose some threat to developing civilizations and neophyte game units, but this threat is minimal and can be, with little effort, avoided entirely by saving and reloading from a point prior to all barbarian-inspired disasters. Rather than treating (and valuing) the barbarians as an oppositional force, dedicated game players are much more likely to attempt to develop their early civilizations with the barbarians' aid.

This cooperative use of barbarians is vital to gaining a foothold in *Civilization* games played at the highest difficulty levels, where the computer-controlled civilizations inevitably attain very large and dangerous early leads in city production and development. Striking a lucky goody hut or two can mean the difference between surviving the game's early years or being quickly overrun by an aggressive adjacent civilization.

Realizing this, the computer-controlled civilizations seek out (and destroy) the goody huts very quickly, with races between civilizations often ensuing not to avoid confrontations with barbarians but to secure them for their own units.[22] There are also other subtle benefits of having barbarians on the map—for example, improving the expertise of your units by sparring with barbarian units and allowing barbarians to fester in unexplored areas to serve as a temporary impedance to the growth of nearby civilizations. However, none of these functions of barbarians *during game play* appear to have any particular significance for critics of in-game barbarian representations. More commonly, text-based descriptions of barbarians—such as those found in game manuals (or game advertising)—are used as justification for assigning values and meanings to play within *Civilization*.

Here, for instance, is such a text-based analysis, drawn from Poblocki (2002):

> Indeed, as an ad informs, "we can match wits with greatest leaders of the world in an all-out quest to build the ultimate empire" (Civ3.com 2002), and we do become one of such nearly divine leaders with a capacity for altering the course of history (hence the popular classification of Civilization in the "you are the god" genre). The *telos*, however, is well known. If in the case of Hegel it was the Prussian state . . . , the fetish-object of Meier's fantasies is the "ultimate empire," the state that resembles most the end product of all human advancement, namely the United States of America.[23]

Text-based descriptions of game units, however, whether appearing in game-supported or supplementary publications—even when appearing as nominatives within the game itself—fail to reveal the manner in which those units are used during play and, as a result of that use, given value and meaning by players. It is well known, for instance, that game players commonly eschew written rules and instructions in favor of more direct and immediate play as a means of determining game goals. And among dedicated game players, the more barbarian-like "Indians" (e.g., Iroquois) are usually considered more advantageously played than the (assumedly) less barbarian-like Americans.

IN THE BACK OF THE BACKSTORIES

Civilization game elements—such as barbarians in early game play and nuclear power in late game play—are obviously interpreted and valued differently by game players than by those who find embedded in the *Civiliza-*

tion games a set of values and meanings existing prior to and apart from game play. These embedded values and meanings can then be understood as a sort of ideological "backstory" to which gamers need not—and most often do not—adhere.

In the previous chapter, I have made the rather contentious claim that game backstories generally have no real relevance to computer game play and, in particular, inhibit, rather than determine, play within computer strategy games. This claim recognizes the degree to which (re)play deconstructs and revalues signs and symbols that are, in other contexts, more conventionally assigned value and meaning. As such, this claim is intended to apply not to *Civilization* alone but to the larger class of computer games that evoke repeated and recursive play. At least one well-known game designer, Raph Koster, in his keynote presentation to the Austin Game Conference (2003), applies a similar argument to concerns that play within *Grand Theft Auto* results in players learning that game's embedded "ethical implications."

> This is why gamers are dismissive of the ethical implications of games—They don't see *"get a blowjob* from a hooker, then *run her over."* They see *a power-up.*[24]

However, there remains an important point unaddressed: what about those aspects of game play that might, with or without conscious intent, replicate preexisting social and cultural values? Sociocultural criticism, after all, may confuse the superficialities of game labels with the underlying mechanisms of game structures; but those game structures might nevertheless still be indicative of some ideological bias originating in some other context. Should all civilizations in the game, for instance, function according to the cultural identity of a single civilization (e.g ., Poblocki's "ultimate empire," mentioned in the preceding section), then claims of ideological bias might well re-emerge.

> The [perfidy] of *Civilization*'s cultural imperialism . . . sneaks into players' own activities, penetrating as deep as their own reconstructed body . . .
>
> The history of Western civilization is to a very high extent a history of the camouflage of power and the means of coercion . . . It is always difficult to spot power in the concept of culture . . . but in strategy computer games such as *Civilization* power is almost invisible because, at least at the level of rhetoric, it belongs to us.[25]

I have so far claimed that patterns and rules governing an aesthetic of play can be observed through the design and redesign of computer games; and I have given examples of this process at work in the evolution of the *Civilization* game series. Let us suppose now that this aesthetic of play is not merely at the root of game design and play but also at the root of cultural bias, power, and "coercion."

For instance, while barbarians are not rightfully considered as a defining opposition to the human player in *Civilization*, other computer-controlled civilizations *are* placed in this sort of opposition. An undeniable theme in the game and its play is, then, a theme of opposition and conflict. Likewise, the most common manner in which the game is played, valued, and analyzed by its most dedicated players is through a systems-based approach that, during recursive play, exhibits an obvious debt to the methods and assumptions of positivist science.

Within the rules and nature of human play, are there seeds of opposition and contextualization that, in their recursive application, create a "culturally biased" form of abstract thought? Or is some distorted aesthetic of play directly imposed on an otherwise culturally neutral cognitive template? There is even the possibility that the vagaries of play become irrevocably intertwined with the backstories of prevailing cultural contexts during the exercise of games as "configurative practices."[26]

> The hacker communities and digital game scenario sites suggest that the awareness of game rules—and the urge to rewrite them—often subverts the games' standing rules governing the way a game can be configured, but they also exceed the rules' ability to configure the operator's paths of thought. Such discourse includes discussion of the aesthetic qualities of the rules themselves . . . This is the two-way process of configuration—operator on game, game on operator—that digital game studies will have to address in the years ahead.[27]

Thus, regardless of how themes of power might get into our play—through ourselves or through others—these themes of power may yet seduce us.

It is, in fact, tempting to see the evolution of the *Civilization* series—from its earliest MS-DOS beginnings, through the feature creep and increasingly sophisticated multiplayer implementations of the past decade, into the condensed and streamlined package of its most recent PlayStation 3 (PS3) edition—as a sort of microcosm of the evolution of computer games as whole:

from geeky spreadsheets to social media platforms to a sleekly commercialized mass-produced products. Yet, it is remarkable, during that evolution, how little the basic form of the game itself has changed.

Probably the single most radical difference between the PC version of *Civ* and the PS3 version (*Civilization Revolution*, 2008), for instance, is the necessity of playing the latter through a console interface. But this transformation, like moving *Zelda* from old to new (Wii) controllers,[28] has little impact, once mastered, on the feel and play of the game. While game play has been considerably shortened inside code changes for the PS3, the basic form of the computer game—and its play—scales down (and up) extremely well. The same sequences and processions of game objects are familiar in the PS3 version; there are simply recognizable fewer of these. The most affective difference is the visual presentation of the game, which benefits in most respects from the more sophisticated graphics of the PS3 hardware. But these graphic embellishments fall on the side of content rather than form and are eventually perceived, during repeated play, as a superficial— even, at moments, disruptive—change; and these superficial trappings of the game form are largely disregarded during the inevitable saves and reloads and recursions and replays that mark the normal progression from novice to expert *Civilization* player.

Noticeably, the newest version of *Civilization* is, if anything, more likely than before to be the target of cultural studies and critiques. The offending superficialities—barbarians, bombs, and backstories of history—are again omnipresent; and this time, the context of their presentation is less complex and detailed and, thus, offers less depth to explore and fewer masteries to achieve in rebuttal of an overly quick and facile interpretation of game themes and narratives.

IS PLAY CIVILIZED?

I can make no more telling argument against the assertions of cultural studies and critical theory than to observe that while games (and "fun") exhibit important cultural differences, characteristics of play appear quite similar across cultures—and, in many respects, across species.[29] And therein a line can be drawn in the sand of current computer game theory between those who would claim that the underlying mechanisms of games and game structures are determined by external factors (narratives among them) and those who would claim that the fundamental mechanisms of play and play structures more accurately reflect their indelibly stamped and now internally fixed biological origins. This is, of course, not a new line[30] (sounding, as it does, suspiciously like the old nature-nurture saw). However, it does allow me to mount some response to those who maintain that these issues are indeterminable.

> I concur with Myers that a user's level of experience informs the likelihood of his or her drawing on internal or external referents while making sense of *Civilization*. However, I would stress that the point is not that either the novice or the expert is more "right" about the meaning of *Civ*. The crucial issue is that the user's level of experience (which will alter as a consequence of play) will constitute the interpretive frame for that user. Furthermore, this shows that the meaning of *Civilization*—whatever it might be—is neither universal, nor static.[31]

On the contrary, expert analysis is indeed more "right" in that the expert analysis is more *complete*. Expert analysis contains and surmounts novice analysis. Yet the meanings and values derived by the novice are derived by the same meaning-making process as those derived by the expert. This formal meaning-making process is both universal and—at least within the bounds of some biologically determined evolutionary time clock—intractable.

Simply put, experts are more capable of generating desired game objects than are novices: they are demonstrably and objectively better *at winning the game*. After extended and recursive play within a game, game object values and meanings increasingly narrow into values and meanings that are more functionally valid (instrumental), more completely realized, and more definitively determined by the game system and code than by the culture in which the game play and player reside. Thus, while a cultural studies perspective might claim a convergence of values based on shared cultural contexts, I would equally claim a convergence of values based on similar game-playing experiences. These play experiences, channeled by game code and interface, eventually trump all other, non-game-related influences *inside the game*.

If play serves as a deconstructive process—and if replay serves even more so—then frequent and dedicated players of computer strategy games will be, over time, increasingly less likely to interpret or be affected by games as cultural statements, either consciously or unconsciously. Play and replay would be, in effect, a *de*-culturalization (or, if you prefer, de-civilization) process.

If, on the other hand, culturalists are right, then frequent and dedicated players of computer games are precisely the group mostly likely to be, over time, indoctrinated by the cultural values embedded in game texts, and they are therefore the group mostly likely to exhibit cognitive and behavioral changes to that effect, regardless of the in-game consequences of these changes. I know of no way to adjudicate this claim other than that already offered: play the game and see who wins.

CHAPTER 9

Social Play

The more you tighten your grip,
the more star systems will slip through your fingers.

—Princess Leia, *Star Wars* (1977)

The most significant development in computer game play over the past quarter century has been the rapid ascension of multiplayer games and game designs, or MMOs. The best-known commercial success story in this genre is, of course, *World of Warcraft* (WoW). WoW and the rest of the current crop of MMOs remain firmly based on the fundamental mechanics of the paper-and-pencil role-playing game *Dungeons & Dragons*. And as such, these games reflect the same forms and processes of play outlined earlier.[1] Yet it often seems that they claim to offer something more.

In *The Nature of Computer Games,* I emphasized the potential of one of the most popular and long-lived computer role-playing games at that time, *Might and Magic (M&M),* to expand its social context.

> As of 2001, there were gathering plans to adapt the *M&M* games to an online, multiplayer environment (*Legends of Might and Magic*). This would involve the creation of a MUD-like context, which would be a natural and congruous expansion of the role-playing genre's basic semiotic form.[2]

Reflecting back, however, that analysis seems naive. For while *Everquest* (1999) and *Ultima Online* (1997) have already been—and continue to be, in their own fashion—successful, the *Might and Magic* franchise had already reached its peak of popularity at the time of my analysis, and it subsequently faded and virtually folded. Nevertheless, the basics of the *M&M* role-playing game design, as carried forth online by Blizzard's *World of Warcraft* and (in planning as of 2009) Bioware's closely analogous *Knights of the Old Republic,* demonstrate that much of the appeal of computer role-playing games remains, broadly put, multiplayer and social. About that, I am not surprised.

I am surprised about some other things. Since I was then—while playing *M&M* in 2001—and am now focused on the nature of play as a cognitive function, I am relatively surprised (and somewhat dismayed) to watch computer game studies and analysis, buoyed by the rise of enormously profitable Internet-based MMOs, increasingly promote the notion that computer game play is most fundamentally a cooperative social activity.[3] This notion is, of course, entirely consonant with similar notions, already discussed, promoting the benefits of good and "functional" play.[4] And based on the analysis here, these paired notions are equally misleading.

> The sociologically-anthropologically oriented tradition of MMORPG and its social aspects is usually related to themes that can be located in what Hakken (1999) calls the microsocial level . . . These studies widely assume that MMORPGs are social spaces . . . As a corollary this tradition usually takes for granted the nature of the individual player as a social being.[5]

WoW—as the now prototypical example of MMOs—offers numerous opportunities for cooperative social play (which usually simply means playing "nice" with others), yet this play, like play in all similar games, might be best attributed either to a game design that forces social grouping in order to accomplish game goals or to what appears to be a common human tendency to establish social relationships without regard to any particular game context or goal or desire to play.

In this inclination toward the social, players of online games might be considered similar to users of MySpace or Facebook or other more generic communications networks, where outside-game relationships dominate and motivate in-game behaviors. Yet games are a special sort of software, and play is a special sort of behavior; and in many instances, neither is explained well with reference to desires for or benefits of group play. Indeed, in *WoW* and its related clones, despite the emphasis on social play, most players play most often alone.[6]

Nevertheless, the inclination to design computer games for social play has been present since very early in video game development and history,[7] although the mechanics that made these designs possible were difficult to achieve without the parallel development of computer-mediated communications networks. Now, with such networks commonplace, it is clearly the intent of many computer game designers to include social play as a meaningful component of computer game play. It is not clear, however, that social play contributes to the experience of computer game play as a unique aesthetic form.

Because computer game play relies so fundamentally on sensory mechanisms and habituated response (i.e., its *interface*), social play within computer games is commonly filtered through some previous realization of locomotor play. This fundamental reliance on bodily mechanics is at least somewhat similar to the experience of reading, insofar as all language systems reference visceral experiences of the human body within three-dimensional space.[8] While playing computer games (unlike reading text/hypertext) may avoid direct reference to language, computer game play cannot avoid reference to these more fundamental schemata or to the cognitive mechanisms that enable and empower them. The presence of other players can refine this reference perhaps, but that presence cannot by itself avoid the interactive and visceral components of computer game play.

For this reason, it seems reasonable to construct an explanation of computer game social play as an extension of computer game individual play, rather than to characterize that individual play as a fragmentary and incomplete version of social play. Indeed, individual computer game play often serves as an antithetical substitute for social play, with video game software often taking the role of (an absent) human opponent.

> Play is older than culture, for culture, however inadequately defined, always presupposes human society, and animals have not waited for man to teach them their playing. We can safely assert, even, that human civilization has added no essential feature to the general idea of play.[9]

In general, the experience of computer game play does not seem to necessarily emerge from social action but, rather, becomes often located within social action through purposeful game design.

SOCIAL PLAY CONTEXTS

Here, in order to better understand the fundamentals of social play and to better understand the relationship between social and individual play, I would like to examine common characteristics of online social play contexts—particularly those distinguished by cooperative and competitive

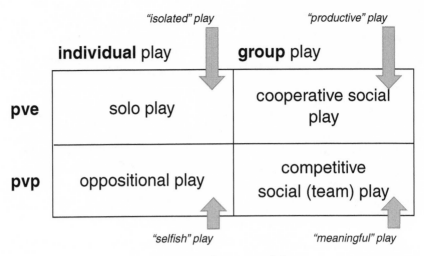

Figure 9.1. Social contexts of play

behaviors in MMOs. These contexts are widely (by players and by designers) represented by the categories of player versus environment (PvE) and player versus player (PvP). While these categories are not mutually exclusive, I will examine them according to the rough configuration in figure 9.1.

PvP combat is often described and treated pejoratively within persistent online communities—that is, as "griefing." Community-based analysis then reproduces these values by emphasizing the negative qualities of competitive play and, simultaneously, the positive qualities of cooperative play— for example, its "productiveness"—as does the following statement from a review of Taylor's (2006) study of *EverQuest* players.

> In short, MMOGs have served as avant-garde prototypes for the online social spaces more and more of us are electing to inhabit, and players are the first to understand how integrating with a computer world allows us to subject our social lives to the same efficiencies that govern our work time and make it seem rational and productive.[10]

This position eventually results in a theoretical denigration of more disruptive and competitive play and distinguishes cooperative play as a more natural and proper extension of individual play. Yet this assumption reflects a disregard—or, perhaps more harmfully, a misrepresentation—of the degree to which competitive play tends to appear and re-appear in a variety of game contexts, regardless of designer intent.

If we position competitive play—among individuals and groups—as a systematic feature of play, then similar formal properties can be observed within cooperative play. And either behavior—cooperative or competitive—can be explained in terms of the systemic manner in which it explores, manipulates, and, over time, transforms the game system.

PvE

"Player versus environment" best describes the play of those single-player games that have been, within the past decades, transformed into today's MMOs. Almost twenty years of *Ultima* single-player games, for instance, preceded the release of *Ultima Online* in 1997. By the time *EverQuest* appeared (in 1999), the computer RPG genre had solidified into a set of design characteristics that could be traced back to early *Dungeons & Dragons* rules sets (1974) and the manipulation of figurines and models within fantasy wargame derivatives such as *Warhammer* (1987).

Under these influences, the computer RPG genre remains marked by two basic components: (1) the creation of a character governed by pre-existing rules and (2) the interactions of that character within a common set of rules. A simplified, linguistic-based model of this process might, for instance, represent a role-playing game as a language system. Playable characters would then be subsets of this rules-based system: grammatically correct sentences. And RPG players are given templates for character structures similar to the basic templates governing sentence structures: a character-creation syntax.

Within the original *Advanced Dungeons & Dragons* (1977) game system, this syntax consisted of seven "basic characteristics": strength, intelligence, wisdom, dexterity, constitution, charisma, and comeliness. All properly constructed characters (well-formed sentences) assigned a bounded value to each of these characteristics. The resulting character array—similar to semantic values chosen during sentence construction—varied slightly from player to player. As a result, each properly constructed character occupied a unique position within the game's multidimensional array of all possible characters. Game play subsequently determined the contextual value of each character in comparison with (or in opposition to) other game characters (or alternative arrays).[11]

Role-playing games remained novel and engaging only to the extent that their play allowed exploration of these character relationships. And in computer games, it is largely immaterial whether these relationships specifically involve other human players. More important, perhaps, is that computer game players assume that they do.

During much of the early history of computer role-playing games, players played in relative social isolation, reacting only to the intricacies of the game system and the variety of character potentials embedded in that system. This sort of play context is then central to the PvE theme and implies an oppositional relationship between game player and game software (or code), with software playing the role of (an imagined) human opponent. Within current MMOs, PvE play now includes groups of players engaged in cooperative attempts to achieve the same or similar game goals.

All PvE play, whether practiced by individuals or groups, remains a meaning-making process that determines values and meanings for game objects; to this end, this process requires an active series of character oppositions during play. The collective history of these oppositions is then used to contextualize each perceptually unique character within an increasingly ordered set of values. These values are continuously weighed and refined with reference to the consequences of in-game interactions, yet they can at times—for example, when narratives are imposed on game play—also include values and meanings imported from external sources. That is, players may assign a low value to a certain character based on game play but may nevertheless highly value that same character for its "aesthetic" value (i.e., as a "concept" character).

In most cases, however, character values and meanings correlate closely with in-game performances, establishing a hierarchy of characters that does not differ greatly from one player to the next. Because this meaning-making process closely parallels the establishment of social hierarchies outside game play, PvE play is formally similar to what appears to be a natural human process: exploring and valuing social relationships. In computer game PvE play, however, this process of assigning contextual values can take place without, strictly speaking, any human contact.

PvP

As technology increasingly has allowed simultaneous and participatory play, the oppositional relationships explored during PvE have become increasingly dependent on other players' presence and choices. Initially, and in parallel with board and card games and most sports, these oppositional relationships result in markedly competitive play. The inclination to design for this competitive tendency among players was present even in early single-player games, where the mechanics of keeping score—or, for instance, hot-seat implementations of turn-based formats—allowed players to value their characters and performances in comparison with the characters and performances of other players.

MMO players distinguish strongly (and emotionally) between these two contexts of play: cooperative and competitive, PvE and PvP. This becomes most obvious in terms of how closely character values come to represent *self* values in these two different play contexts. In general, PvP'ers tend to be much more concerned about the relationship between their in-game characters and their out-of-game selves than are PvE'ers.

There are two clear indications of this exaggerated identification of self with character among PvP players: the tone and topics of in-game communications and, related, the degree to which PvP'ers promote some form of *inequity aversion*.

PvP COMMUNICATIONS

One of the more obvious and distinguishing characteristics of PvP play—particularly in comparison to PvE play—is the energetic conversation (smack talk) that takes place among players. In comparison to PvE communications, in-game communications among PvP players tends to occur more often as a direct result of the consequences of play, is more predictable as to precisely when during play it will occur, and more often than not concerns the rules of play when it does occur. In contrast, conversations among PvE players commonly exist only as a (often distant) back channel to a more immediate in-game play experience.

When PvP players communicate with their online opponents, that communication plays a significant role in assigning personal character values. Aside from a certain amount of nervous banter and a brief feeling-out process, PvP players talk most often and predictably to their opponents just after they have been defeated in combat and "die."

Because virtually all MMOs determine character oppositions and their consequences according to rules sets that are largely hidden from players, the quantitative meaning of individual combat remains uncertain, leading to necessarily qualitative and social-based interpretations of character values. Therefore, in order to maintain a positive character value, it is vital that players immediately—and publicly—rationalize any indication of weakness or defeat. MMO combat winners occasionally assert their superiority, but these are ritualized and generic comments (e.g., "pwnd!"), without reference to specific elements of game play. MMO combat losers, on the other hand, are much more likely (and much quicker) to point out any inequities that could be attributed to their loss: computer lag, imbalanced game design, and such.

Losing players tend to isolate and criticize specific game elements; winning players tend to generalize their winning performances across broader contexts—often extending the values and meanings derived from in-game play in real-world contexts (e.g., through online forums and message boards). For both winners and losers, these communications establish over time a common and shared set of values based on prioritizing inequity aversion.

PvP VALUES

"Inequity aversion" promotes the assumption that the game is fair and that all PvP combatants have equal opportunities—regardless of characters played—to "win." Any variation in winning outcomes is then attributed to the single aspect of play considered to be uncontrolled and undetermined by the game rules: the game player. This is, of course, a more popular assumption among consistent PvP winners than among consistent PvP losers. However, both winners and losers share this common value. It is just that the winning players, with a higher status granted by their in-game winning characters, are normally louder, more persistent, and more persuasive in its assertion.

With this principle of inequity aversion widely held, there are then two generic arguments presented at the end of any decisive PvP battle. The losers' argument goes something like this: "You killed me in combat only because of game-related factor X." To which the winner replies, "Game-related factor X has little to no significance in the outcome, since that outcome is much more dependent on player skill." Neither of these positions is ever subsequently justified (though the attempt is often made), yet each continues to be supported and promoted by those whose self-valuations would most benefit from its adoption.

These same values and meanings are seldom topics of discussion and debate during PvE play. PvE players are much more willing to allow others to "win" by whatever means (equitable or inequitable)—insofar as that winning does not affect their own self-valuations. As a result, hierarchies of PvE character values are slightly different (i.e., more idiosyncratic) than those constructed solely with reference to PvP activities. Over the course of a long-lived MMO, these values can diverge significantly, resulting in two separate cultures of play. Importantly, however, of the two, PvP value determinations remain more accurate and more indicative of underlying game rules and mechanics, due to their constant testing in game-related competitive contexts.

Based on this realization and on the assumption that an important systemic function of play is to explore the mechanics of the game (or any similarly complex system), PvP play—in which players are put into direct and immediate opposition with one another—provides a quicker, more accurate, and more definitive set of in-game character values and meanings than does PvE play. This determination process is simultaneously a source of satisfaction for individual PvP'ers and a genuine boon for game designers—as an aid in discovering bugs, learning of unintended consequence of complicated rules sets, and so forth.

If, indeed, the values determined and the meanings made during PvP play offer a more complete and thorough analysis of the game system than do the values and meanings resulting from PvE play, it would seem to follow that PvE play can be reasonably conceptualized as a distorted and incomplete version of PvP play—and, further, that much of those supposed dysfunctions associated with strongly individual, competitive, and "grief"-related play are, in fact, positive (and otherwise unachievable) functions when viewed within the context of the game system as a whole.

This is perhaps the most compelling reason to assume that oppositional play (*anti*-play) is a fundamental and default condition of human play—not because computer game players seem to desire it more often (many of them do not), but because it has as an important adaptive function for larger systems. However, simply prioritizing oppositional play over cooperative play does not entirely clarify the relationship between the two. It remains unclear as to whether competition among *groups* or competition among *individuals* is more common and critical to an understanding of competitive play. For, again, just as PvE and cooperative social play are championed within their supportive player communities, there are similarly linked assumptions prioritizing *team-based* PvP.

SOCIAL PLAY THEORY

Clearly, in most play contexts—when observing animal play, for instance—it is relatively easy to distinguish social from individual play. And even in human computer game play, these two forms of play become conceptually intertwined only when computer games also serve as communication devices and, in their communication functions, allow players to share common experiences during play. MMOs currently qualify both as video games and as social communities—though one set of functions may not require and, in fact, may interfere with the other.

Ideally, perhaps, social play within computer role-playing games would extend the liminal qualities of individual play.[12] Turner (1969) has similarly extended his original concept of the liminal—into *communitas*.

> According to Turner, communitas does not engage in active opposition to social structure, but merely appears as "an alternative and more 'liberated' way of being socially human". . . It is "a loving union of the structurally damned pronouncing judgment on normative structure and providing alternative models for structure" . . . In its most open form, a liminal event reveals a "model of human society as a homogeneous, unstructured communitas, whose boundaries are ideally coterminous with those of the human species."[13]

Communitas, as just defined, is uncommon within MMOs. Online computer games promoting widespread social play generate strict social hierarchies with strong normative guidelines, often only peripherally related to game goals. These hierarchical groups—guilds, fellowships, kinships, and such—tend to restrict computer game object-value relationships much as simulations do. As a result, depending on your point of view, they either protect or prevent individual players from fully accessing a computer game (anti-)aesthetic.

The primary function of computer game social play, then, is to control and deny the experience of self. That is, social play tends to require, as does the simulation, a common set of rules and, correspondingly, a predetermined and fixed set of object-value relationships. This significantly affects game play among members of a social group and becomes most obvious in comparing the consequences of PvE and PvP play.

Social play, in order to maintain a common set of player goals, is more likely to impose sanctions on PvP behavior (e.g., constructing false or "fixed" competitions) than to pursue those competitions without bounds, thus limiting the degree to which individuals can explore the game space, rules, and system. Avoiding the consequences of an anti-play in this fashion requires that social play substitutes social benefits for the more isolated pleasures of individual play and the liminal; accordingly, most currently successful MMO designs manufacture and package the pleasures of play as "loot." In loot-based games, social groups can offer their members information concerning game mechanics, quest walk-throughs, "twinking," and various other boons (depending on the genre and setting of the game) that, in terms of the discussion here, solidify object-value relationships without threat to social cohesion. This means that some members—the majority—of an online social play group are not required to undergo the same habituation process as other members, and for that reason, the former may experience the computer game (anti-)aesthetic solely as a text aesthetic.

This phenomenon, I daresay, also marks much current computer game analysis, which interprets social and cultural strictures on game play as a form of creativity—for example, as a source of "user-created" content.

> There is no culture, there is no game, without the labor of the players. Whether designers want to acknowledge it fully or not, MMOGs *already are* participatory sites (if only partially realized) by their very nature as social and cultural spaces.[14] (italics in original)

For those who would observe and record the interpretative practices of players as social activities reflecting shared cultural values, user-created content is an important outcome of play that can be explained and understood with reference to other, similarly located social and cultural phenomena. For those who would locate the phenomenon of play in individual cognition rather than common society, however, user-created content is a largely predetermined feature of a particular game form—that is, a looseness of rules—that allows games to be configured and therein exploited by social groups and pressures. The resulting "user-created" content, like all other rules-based structures within the game, can then engage and empower individual and anti-play only through its opposition and, ultimately, denial.

SUMMARY AND IMPLICATIONS

Analysis of two well-defined contexts of online social play—PvP and PvE—within the shared game space of MMOs offers at least three potential explanations of the relationship between individual play (particularly individual and competitive play) and social or group play (particularly social and cooperative play).

The first explanation—or hope—might be that these contexts of play could coexist, separate but equal; but this is immediately contradicted by widespread and ongoing conflicts among PvE and PvP players. There are clearly different goals and values associated with PvE and PvP play, despite these two sharing the same game space, rules, and, in many cases, players. One or another, it seems, needs to be assigned precedence in practice and in theory.

Another explanation—the most positive and the most conventional—

prioritizes social and cooperative play (primarily within PvE contexts) as a more advanced and mature form of what is initially individual, oppositional, and selfish play. This explanation would eventually subsume all oppositional and individual play within those cooperative groups and game designs that create and maintain social order. It would likewise promote and prioritize teamwork, group coordination, and individual sacrifice over self-reliance, independence, and self-interest.

An immediate difficulty with this second position, however, is that the value and meaning determinations available through supposedly more "mature" and "advanced" forms of play are often less satisfying to players and less useful to designers than those resulting from more "primitive" forms of play. Further, attempting to guide and control oppositional play through social institutions and mechanisms simply doesn't work very well. Self-motivated and solo play is quite common at all levels of MMO play, among beginner and advanced players, in both PvE and PvP contexts. And individual and oppositional play most often occurs without regard to any rules or designs that attempt to limit or channel its effects; individual play appears, for want of a better word, incorrigible.

Cooperative play and tightly knit groups of players may partially distort and sublimate the functions of self-oriented and oppositional play, or social pressures or game designs may temporarily channel player self-interests and activities from direct and immediate oppositions (e.g., 1v1 combat) to other, more complex methods of determining character value (e.g., team-based competitions). However, neither of these factors eliminate the persistence of individual play in MMOs, nor does either significantly alter the self-centered nature of individual play whenever and wherever it occurs.

A third explanation—the most likely—is that individual and competitive play is core and fundamental to an understanding of human play behavior—much more so than cooperative and social play. In other words, human play, regardless of context or group, can be best explained and understood as originating within individual players—in and according to *self*. The most important and revealing consequences of selfish play, however, only become apparent when viewed in the context of larger groups and systems—and, somewhat paradoxically, these larger groups and systems tend to negatively value the motivations and behaviors associated with individual and selfish play. It is not inconceivable, however—or unprecedented—that individual self-interests might be at the core of larger group and system functions, sustenance, and survivability.

In economics, for instance, John Nash came to a similar conclusion regarding the relationship between competitive and cooperative market behaviors. In economic game theory, the so-called Nash program assumes that all market-driven cooperative games can be reduced to a non-cooperative (competitive) form.

> The most important new contribution of Nash (1951) . . . was his argument that this non-cooperative equilibrium concept . . . gives us a complete methodology for analyzing all games.[15]

Since Nash, other economic analyses (e.g., "behavioral finance")[16] have emphasized the degree to which individual, self-determined, and often, as a result, non-rational behaviors explain market outcomes more accurately (and more realistically) than does an assumption of perfect rationality among players.[17] Nevertheless, among theorists most directly concerned with the social outcomes of play—for example, Piaget (1932, 1954)—there is often the implicit assumption that any individual and selfish motives of play are inappropriate and should be subsequently molded into more acceptable social behaviors. Jose Linaza quotes Piaget to make the point that Piaget "at a general level upheld a continuity between all three forms of social behavior (motor, egocentric and cooperative)":

> . . . one must be aware of laying down the law; for things are motor, egocentric, and social all at once. . . . rules of cooperation are in some respects the outcome of rules of coercion and of motor rules.[18]

Clearly, the popularity of social software and social games has been one of the major success stories in the gaming industry over the past decade, and WoW represents an undeniable high point in that trend. Yet many characteristics of WoW—and other similar online games—seem in conflict with an individually located and biologically determined play. In particular, the persistence of online social communities—including those cultural assumptions, rules, and social pressures that sustain play through the indefinite extension of game form—seems counter to an otherwise and elsewhere fragile, fragmented, and fleeting human play.

In promoting group-oriented play behavior, MMO design and analysis tend to denigrate the persistent and incorrigible features of individual play. Yet, despite all their conflicts, PvE and PvP players share the same joys and immediacies of individual play, before and beyond the influence of subsequent player groupings. These shared pleasures are found in common elements of the game that social and cultural analyses often take for granted: the embedded mechanics of the game interface, the analogical sensation of movement through three-dimensional space, and those private and idiosyncratic fantasies evoked during the game's initial process of character creation.

Similarly, there are strongly shared distastes among MMO PvE and PvP players. One of the most telling of these is their mutual desire to avoid "permadeath."[19] For while "death" is, of course, the most common result of a computer game player's inability to achieve game goals, this pseudo-death is entirely representational and primarily serves as a way to limit extended play (e.g., in arcade games) and provide performance-related feedback (in all games). In action-based video games, players bounce back quickly from multiple deaths and, at the end of the game, are none the worse for wear. Within role-playing games, however, the creation of a character is a more involved and more significant portion of the game experience than it is within arcade and action games—and designers greatly extend this process of character creation so that RPG characters slowly change and "level up" over time.

The most repulsive portion of the penalty of permadeath in MMOs is that the dead character, if still valuable in some way, needs to be re-created ("re-rolled") from the beginning of the game. Aside from the great amount of time involved, this is an unacceptable consequence to most players—solo and social—for a common aesthetic reason: enjoyable game play is a meaning-making process based on assigning values to oppositional relationships, including those relationships in which one game object or character is so highly valued over some other that the lower-value character can only "die" as a consequence of that opposition. But if such death-causing oppositions are just as likely, just as informative, and just as valuable (i.e., just as "meaningful" and aesthetically pleasing) as any other, then assigning a particularly onerous consequence to one particular sort of relationship greatly increases the difficulty of determining the proper values for all possible relationships. Indeed, if enjoyable MMO play requires (at least the expectation of) a full exploration of all potential characters and character relationships, then permadeath is overly restrictive to this end. Permadeath therein becomes an incongruous MMO design feature that disrupts the normal and most enjoyable flow and consequences of play within the contexts of both cooperative and competitive play.

Thus, even if we firmly situate PvE as cooperative play and PvP as competitive play, both still involve character creation according to a fixed (and often identical) set of rules. Both involve assigning value and meanings to game characters and game objects based on their in-game relationships and the consequences of interactive play. Both result in a (pseudo-)social hierarchy that arranges and values characters in a manner similar to those values and arrangements found in external social contexts. And both, for all these reasons, find pleasure—and displeasure—in similar game design features, including a mutual abhorrence of character permadeath in MMOs.

"Productive" social play in MMOs would channel individual play into forms that are stable, predictable, and comfortable but also less diverse and less accurate in determining game values based on oppositional relationships. Therefore, currently popular MMO game designs, particularly those promoting cooperative play, operate most fundamentally as a means of social *control*—and this function must be weighed heavily against their more productive outcomes.

Yet, simultaneously, an important distinction between game experiences and literary experiences is the degree to which the latter are essentially personal while the former are always potentially social. To play is to play *with* some idea, object, or person; and as computer game technologies have evolved, it has become not only increasingly common but also increasingly appropriate to incorporate multiplayer components into computer game designs. While computer games may function most fundamentally as private experiences of self-construction, they also have the potential, unrealized by literature during the process of reading, to function as social experiences as well.

Therefore, in order to develop a comprehensive theory of play, analysis of MMOs must more clearly delineate the role of individual play within social game system design and evolution. To this end, social play will need to be re-conceptualized to include its apparently derivative and potentially negative influences on the adaptive functions of individual and oppositional play.

To this end, enter Twixt.

CHAPTER 10

City of Heroes

The center cannot hold.

    —William Butler Yeats, "The Second Coming" (1920)

I am—but only sort of—Twixt. Twixt is a character I played, on and off, for four years (2004–8) inside the MMO *City of Heroes/City of Villains* (*CoH/V*).

CoH/V was originally designed by Cryptic Studios and released in 2004 for the PC by NCsoft. Following that release, the game went through several revisions ("issues"); these issues—released at least once a year—added game content as well as tweaking and refining game rules. The original design team from Cryptic Studios and the primary game designer, Jack Emmert, sold their interests in the game to NCsoft in 2007.

CoH/V breaks somewhat from the traditional MMO model in not offering a conventional (swords and sorcery) fantasy setting; in all other important respects, however, *CoH/V* is extremely typical of contemporary MMO designs. During *CoH/V* play, players choose and costume a superhero (or supervillain), who, over the course of play, improves in powers and abilities. In *CoH/V*, as in other MMOs, character actions depend on "basic characteristics" that determine a character's interactions with other characters and with the game environment. Through continued play (and a continued monthly fee), basic characteristics increase in value and potency—characters "level up"—and the higher-level and more powerful characters unlock additional game content and play experiences.

I would like, here, to use my experience playing Twixt, in some detail, as a basis for examining fundamental issues concerning MMO play and, in particular, the relationship between game rules and social and individual play inside MMOs. This requires a review of the *CoH/V* game design and its game players, which I take as representative of computer games and players in general.

The *CoH/V* game code—the rules—establishes multiple winning conditions (most desired game objects)—some simple to achieve, others complex. In the *CoH/V* design, the most obvious, basic, and desirable game object—a high-level character—can be achieved through either group or solo play.

> On the one hand, this is a MMP. I believe that some of the best features of the game shine when players join forces with other players. On the other hand, I've always believed that part of our game's strength is the ability for a player to log on for a half hour, have fun, then log off. If a mission requires a team up, players spend a lot of time simply organizing. The quick fun element dissipates . . . Simply put: if a player wants to do something solo, it should be CHOICE. Teaming shouldn't be required, but rather encouraged.[1]

Because of this explicit choice by the original game designers, *CoH/V* offers one of the better opportunities among MMOs to compare group and individual play without the game code skewing that comparison toward either context. A necessary first step toward this comparison, then, is to distinguish between play activities characteristic of a group and those characteristic of individuals within *CoH/V*. Inside an MMO, what exactly must—and can— players do alone?

First, as is the case with all computer games, MMO players are required to master the physical interface separating them from the game code and subsequent conceptual play. This is not an insignificant obstacle, and it is one that players must negotiate largely isolated and alone, prior to more involved engagement with the MMO community of players. Beyond this necessity, however, object and conceptual play in MMOs like *CoH/V* is also a frequently solo and solitary undertaking by choice.

INDIVIDUAL PLAY: SELF CONSTRUCTION

As I began play in *CoH/V,* my first conceptual task was to figure out where I was and what I was doing: to distinguish my "self"—my avatar—from its surroundings. Until this most basic distinction is made, there is no set of oppositions to use to form a referential context within which further game objects can be valued. The hierarchical process of selecting a *CoH/V* character archetype (a "class"), then powers within that archetype, then enhancements within those powers demands an understanding of the oppositional values of archetypes and powers and enhancements. Yet in the beginning, players do not have the experience or knowledge necessary to distinguish among these, and prior to such a distinction, no meaningful game play can occur.

Therefore, the first question for all players is this one: who am I and who am I *not*? New players must answer this all-important question without much, if any, reference to the game code—simply because they have not yet gained the tools to make such reference.

These new players make their first choices of self and self-construction in reference to *previous* experiences and *other* game contexts than the one in which they find themselves. At this beginning moment, narrative and "back-story" exert their greatest influence on MMO game play and players. *CoH/V* players, for instance, create a self—a superhero—based on what they believe (or desire) a superhero, in general, to be.

The result is that a great number of *CoH/V* superheroes resemble Spiderman, Superman, The Tick, and Mr. Incredible—among others. My first superhero inside the game was "Quag," a rather bland, vaguely military type, whose name was borrowed from a team I had played in another game, a totally unrelated fantasy baseball competition. Soon after Quag, I also created—with my young daughter, who played alongside me for a couple of months—a series of characters modeled after the *Street Fighter* game series: Blanca, Zangief, and the like. None of these characters proved long-lived.

In my case and others, two important factors work against a simple and straightforward replication of out-of-game expectations inside a computer game. The first is the nature of play itself, which evokes an *anti*-ness resulting more characteristically in continuous variation than in unembellished duplication. The second is—in the particular case of *CoH/V*—a relatively unique design component: its detailed system for costume creation.

Within *CoH/V*, the process of selecting superhero characteristics, powers, and enhancements is separate from that of selecting superhero sex, height, weight, costume, and physical appearance. These latter selections, unlike the former, have no real effect on instrumental game play.

CoH/V offers players an enormous variety of costume selections—much more so than competing MMOs, which more often tie avatar appearance and gear to the relative strength or level (or *value*) of that avatar within the game context. Though *CoH/V* limits certain costume affectations (e.g., capes and auras) to specific game experiences and contexts, the game code allows even beginning players great latitude in costume creation and thereby makes the costuming process easily accessible to individual and self-motivated play. In fact, the costuming process in *CoH/V* is *necessarily* individual play in that the game's screen for costume selection —its user interface— precludes conversations and interactions with other players.

While Quag was clad in flak vest and combat boots, and while Blanca was green-skinned and monstrous, my subsequent costume creations were increasingly idiosyncratic. These remained influenced, in part, by my past experiences and expectations of superhero attire, but these creations and choices became more often influenced and determined by the mechanics and potentials of the *CoH/V* game code. Certain costume choices, for instance, "fit" the game's animated character images more neatly; certain skins and colors were more compatible with the game display, others less so. And whereas my goal in the initial stages of play had been to reproduce the superhero images of others, I eventually became interested in creating a superhero image of *my own*—as did my daughter.

My daughter's "main" character became "Mr. Suave," a rather ugly and random (to my eyes) amalgamation of grayish-bluish costume parts—with tail. And my "main" became Twixt, who, for the next four years, would retain, with subtle variations eventually diminishing some initial garishness, the dark green spandex tights of his origin.

Character costume contests are frequently held in beginning player areas of *CoH/V*. These events are neither provided for nor supported by the game code and are arranged solely through player initiative. During these contests, beginning characters vie with one another for "best costume" prizes, most often awarded by more advanced characters. The decision as to which costume is "best" is left to the whim of the more advanced character(s), and participation in these contests highlights the pecking order between the high and the low within the social hierarchy of the game. Yet participation in these contests—ostensibly to please the tastes of more advanced players—does not imply that beginning players relinquish control over the costuming process. Costumes designed specifically for competitions are usually used once or twice for this purpose only and then discarded. Just as very few players retain initial costume designs based on something other than their own game experiences and valuations, very few players retain a costume designed to accomplish some other player's goal, particularly when that goal is inconsistent with their own personal and aesthetic sense of self.

Over time, the unique sense of self that players gain through character selection and costume design in *CoH/V* does not come from any single costume choice made or the appearance of any particular character created. Rather, players come to identify their in-game selves with their entire stable of characters and costumes, not just the fixed characteristics and appearance of any single one.

Player signatures, such as the following, posted on the *CoH/V* message board forums indicate this clearly.

[NOTABLE CHARACTERS]
HEROES: °Biostem, °Khel'Biostem, °Glacial Gauntlet, °Actuator, °Unbreakable Bones, Biko, °Blue Blade Brother, Bow Knows

VILLAINS: °Sinner-man, °Humanoid Hunter, °Fridge Chick, °Mind-numb, OpFor, °Slabman, °Amelia Hourglass °Is level 50.

Umbral Fist : Dm/Reg Scrap
Umbral Lantern : Fire/Ice Tank
Umbral Paradox : Rad/Psi Def
Umbral Impulse : Elec/Nrg Blast
Umbral Elemental : Earth/Kin Troller
Umbral Astrum: Da/Nrg Tank
Umbral Unleashed: WS
Umbral Luminary: PB

Extended identities such as these establish a sense of self based increasingly less on player-character appearances and increasingly more on game-playing experiences. These experiences, regardless of whether or not they include other players, are both self-directed and self-constructive. In fact, even when promoting an extended self, as in the preceding forum signature examples, players eventually come to identify most often with a single character—a Mr. Suave or a Twixt.

Individual and isolated play within MMOs and within all computer games—using costume creation in *CoH/V* as an exemplar of this play—manipulates, arranges, and values game elements (semiotic objects) in a context of self. This context must necessarily preexist some parts of game play, yet this context is also a significant outcome of game play and, once established, serves as a basis for further in-game valuations.

SOCIAL PLAY: SUPRA-CONTEXTUALIZATION

We saw earlier[2] how a group of researchers, acting in concert, recontextualized the rules of a prisoner's dilemma tournament to more highly value their own play (at the expense of the play of others). I call this process *supra-contextualization*, and it is typical both of advanced individual play in all computer games and, equally, of dedicated social play in MMOs.

CoH/V—again, like all MMOs—motivates group play in several ways. One is by providing tasks within the game that are impossible to accomplish individually. Another is by giving players the freedom to set their own goals. Costume contests, for instance, are examples of player-initiated social play unconnected to any specific game-related tasks or goals.

As a result, social play within MMOGs is frequently *non-instrumental* play, much of which takes place outside the game context entirely. For instance, *CoH/V* supergroups (similar to guilds in other MMOs) maintain independent Web sites, hold special events (both inside and outside the game), and serve as a means for exchanging personal as well as game-related information. In addition, many *CoH/V* supergroups promote role-playing activities that are entirely superfluous to the game code and rules.

However, MMOs and *CoH/V* designs strongly motivate *instrumental* group play as well. Some missions within *CoH/V* cannot be attempted—much less accomplished—by a single player. Other missions cannot be accomplished by certain character classes or are more easily accomplished, with greater rewards, by a group of characters rather than by an individual character. These missions include the game's optional but very rewarding "task forces" (similar to raids in other MMOs) and, at one time, the crowning achievement of the game, reserved for its most advanced and accomplished characters: the defeat of the amoebic monster (the "superboss") Hamidon.

Supergroups

Social group play within *CoH/V* commonly occurs in one of three contexts: (a) pickup groups (PUGs); (b) supergroups; and (c) supra-groups, such as those required to defeat the Hamidon.

Initially, play within *CoH/V*—within the game's tutorial and during initial character/costume creation, for instance—is predominately and purposefully solo play. But soon after the tutorial is completed, PUGs are sought and valued by players. These first groups are randomly selected, include mostly strangers, and, eventually, become a notorious source of frustration and ridicule. Because individual play styles, expectations, and values are often in conflict inside PUGs, PUG game play results in many in-game failures, deaths, and dissatisfactions.

Nevertheless, PUGs remain common in *CoH/V* because they are necessary functionally and because, despite all their problems, they are aesthetically pleasing. As individual play within *CoH/V*—within all games—becomes increasingly less novel over time, group play offers a new game context and, therein, the potential to revalue and reinvigorate individual play. This particular recontextualization, however, comes at a cost.

When solo play within *CoH/V* becomes boring, the solo player can, to increase novelty, either recontextualize the game within an alternative context of self (e.g., create another character or "alt"—which requires, in effect, starting the game over) or revalue the game's semiotic objects—including self—outside the game context entirely (e.g., sell their character on eBay). In pursuing either of these options, players must relinquish, at least in some part, self-constructed game values that have been the primary motivation for their play up to that point.

Group play offers a third option. Groups of all kinds, including PUGs, revalue the individual play context and make it more novel. However, simultaneously, group play limits and restricts the individual play context so that this same novel aesthetic can be provided for *all* members of the group, rather than just one. That is, individual play can still take place in groups; it just then can't be quite so *selfish*.

But, of course, since play is fundamentally selfish, this makes the group play context, particularly the PUG context, ripe for manipulation and subversion by individual players. For instance, sophisticated *CoH/V* players use PUG mechanisms for their own individual goals, regardless of the effect this has on other members of the group. This is most evident in *CoH/V* power-leveling techniques and the use and treatment of "fillers" at upper levels of play.

During power leveling, a low-level character is placed within a high-level group solely in order for that low-level character to benefit from the strongly instrumental play of the high-level characters within the group. During the group play required by power leveling, group values and goals are clearly defined, with no room for individual play variation. Thus, this particular type of group play tends to strongly devalue individual play. This is most true of the character being power leveled, but it is also true of the characters doing the power leveling. The play of these advanced characters is so strongly instrumental and repetitive that the individual play experience becomes associated more closely with work than with play. As a consequence, anyone who wants to "play the game" and have "fun" either avoids power-leveling activities entirely or must be willing to delay that fun until some vague time in the future when all power leveling has been fully accomplished.

Because of peculiarities in the *CoH/V* code, it is also more efficient—again, primarily for power-leveling purposes—to complete certain in-game tasks with a large PUG composed of characters whose "jobs" are simply to be a part of the group and do nothing whatsoever. These characters are commonly called "fillers." Fillers, in fact, need serve only a brief and temporary function: they occupy slots in the PUG at the beginning of some in-game task and then quickly—and sometimes preferably—are dropped or "kicked" from the group.

Beginning *CoH/V* players, of course, have little knowledge of such intricacies of advanced play. Therefore, beginning *CoH/V* players often receive private invitations for group play from advanced players ("blind tells"), accept these invitations, and then are silently and unceremoniously kicked from their play group a short time later. From the beginning player's point of view, this is no doubt rude and antisocial behavior. Seen within the larger context of an anti-aesthetic of play, however, this is simply the sort of thing that should be expected within a computer game design that imposes group play necessities on individual play sensibilities.

In order to avoid these sorts of boorishly selfish play inside groups, new players eventually learn to avoid PUGs in favor of *supergroups*. Supergroups are collections of players known to each other, whose in-game behavior is therefore more predictable and trustworthy than that of members of an anonymous PUG.

While task-oriented *CoH/V* play groups—such as PUGs—are limited to eight members, supergroups may have up to seventy-five members, who can then select among their fellows for help and participation in group-related in-game activities. Even with the average supergroup size being much less than the maximum of seventy-five, some very large supergroups flourished during Twixt's four-year span inside *CoH/V*. But not for long.

Supergroups tend to be unstable—and very susceptible to leader burnout. The more successful supergroups in *CoH/V* provide a predetermined context for group play, which, ideally, diminishes conflicts among individual players. Nevertheless, play within supergroups—regardless of the specifics of group composition—promotes different values than those associated with individual play. And in the case of *CoH/V* supergroups, there are number of specific obligations required of members that become increasingly restrictive to individual play.

CoH/V supergroups, like all similar social groups within MMOs, establish a clearly marked hierarchy, with leaders, captains, lieutenants, and so forth. At the high end of this structure, leaders have the ability to invite members, reject members, and promote members within their ranks. Leaders are also involved—often as a form of individual play—in establishing a set of rules guiding supergroup membership and play. These rules might be very rigid or very loose, but membership within supergroups is not given indiscriminately—and is frequently revoked if and when warranted.

The rules of supergroups maintain a clear distinction between in-group and out-of-group behavior. Establishing common and (when necessary) consensual group values forces supergroup members into a sometimes uneasy and uncomfortable compromise between strongly focused instrumental group play (e.g., power-leveling sessions) and a freer, less restrictive, and more enjoyable play outside the supergroup context entirely.

For the majority of supergroup members, play within supergroups distorts the natural inclination of play to distinguish between self and other. In place of this distinction, group play substitutes values determined and sustained outside the immediacy of individual play—for example, the values associated with "loot" and other in-game awards. This results in a distortion of the aesthetics and pleasures of individual play and, over time, a decrease in the enjoyment of that play—which, in turn, results in the instability and eventual dissolution of supergroups.

Beyond PUGs and supergroups, there is the third type of social context in *CoH/V*, the supra-group, which for a long time (somewhat strangely) proved both more fragile and more sustainable than either of the other two.

The Hamidon and the *Supra*-group

The culminate form of group play within *CoH/V* is the Hamidon raid, restricted to the game's most advanced characters.

> The Hamidon was once a zealous scientist named Hamidon Pasilima. Using hideous dark magic and his own genetic genius, he transformed himself into the god-like monster that would spawn the Devouring Earth and threaten the entire world. Time and again, hundreds of heroes from Paragon City have banded together to defeat the Hamidon whenever it arises.[3]

Defeating the Hamidon might be accomplished by a single large supergroup, but in accordance with the original game design (prior to issue 9, May 2007), the raid was more often open to all advanced players. Defeating the Hamidon might require fifty or more superheroes, and on any given night, the raid might include as many as 200 players. This loose confederation of players, most of whom did not know each other and worked together only for the couple of hours it took to defeat the Hamidon, was a sort of mega-PUG or, perhaps more descriptively, a *supra*-group.

The supra-group supports group play values yet, concurrently, provides many opportunities for individual play. Unlike supergroups, for instance, the Hamidon supra-group formed solely on an ad hoc basis. And, as it turns out, the two fundamental and distinguishing characteristics of the supra-group—its immediacy and its impermanence[4]—are much more conducive to individual play than are the more rigid and rules-based contexts of supergroups.

Social play within the Hamidon raid includes organizing the raid, forming teams prior to the raid, and broadcasting instructions and guidelines during the course of the raid. A small minority of players conducts these activities; and this same cadre of players is likely to simultaneously hold leadership positions within each server's supergroups. For these players, then, the Hamidon raid is very similar to the socially based (but still individually motivated) play of leadership within supergroups.

For the majority of players, however, a supra-group raid on the Hamidon is quite different from a supergroup mission task. Social ties and, correspondingly, social rules are not so strong or so binding in the supra-group as in the supergroup. In fact, players are likely—as encouraged by raid leaders—to ignore supergroup affiliations and form more functional teams appropriate to the task of defeating the Hamidon. Without clearly defined social roles or allegiances, and with a number of different levels of participation available (from leader to kibitzer), many *CoH/V* players choose to join the Hamidon raid as individuals and play solo, while, in effect, playing in unison with many other individual players doing likewise: they play alone together.

Of course, in this large supra-group context, as within PUGs, the anonymity of its members and the looseness of social rules offer many opportunities for individual players to manipulate and subvert group goals. However, because the Hamidon encounter is a temporary (and eternally renewable) in-game task with little meaningful consequences (other than the loot the Hamidon drops), griefing and other sorts of "bad" play are, by *CoH/V* standards, endured much more cheerfully during Hamidon raids than at any other time. One significant contributing factor to such magnanimousness, no doubt, is the relative inability of individual grief play to have much impact on the concerted efforts of such a large group of players. Indeed, the good and tolerating nature of the supra-group arises largely from its invulnerability to individual variations in play. Probably for that reason alone, the Hamidon raid was, for a long time, one of the more popular and widely attended group activities on all *CoH/V* servers. Then the rules—the game code—changed.

In May 2007, with the introduction of issue 9, the *CoH/V* game code changed the Hamidon encounter from an activity requiring the loose cooperation of hundreds of superheroes to a much more tightly structured activity requiring the close cooperation of many fewer superheroes. Immediately, the popularity of the event plummeted.

After May 2007, although the same in-game awards (loot) were available after defeating the Hamidon, players no longer came together on a regular basis to do the deed. With a drastic drop in attendance on all *CoH/V* servers, Hamidon raids became correspondingly less central in *CoH/V* game discussion and lore. Why, then, the change? Based on designer comments, the Hamidon code was changed to avoid the ease with which individual players could annoy (though, again, without much effect) the Hamidon supra-group mass—and, simultaneously, to increase the event's "challenge."

> We wanted to address as many of the common complaints as we could, and also wanted Hamidon raids to be much more dynamic and require a lot more coordination. The Hamidon should represent the pinnacle challenge in the game. We've designed the Hamidon raid around one general strategy, but there should be many different ways to accomplish it. We want everyone involved in a Hamidon raid to be fully participating and not on auto-pilot, following another player around with a power on auto-cast.[5]

Certainly, "challenge" is an important component of computer game design and play.[6] But while the notion of "challenge" is rather straightforward in single-player computer games, it can be a trickier concept in MMOs. "Challenge," like most aesthetically pleasing characteristics of play, originates in regards to *individual* play. Thus, for example, while leaders of *CoH/V* supergroups face significant challenges—as individuals—in creating and maintaining their groups over time, the rank-and-file members of those groups face significantly fewer challenges (and, in fact, commonly seek and enjoy supergroup play precisely for that reason: it's easier).

Many challenging aspects of the original *CoH/V* Hamidon encounter involved individual play: building a proper character, placing that character in the proper position, or simply pushing the proper buttons at the proper time. None of these tasks were overly difficult, but all were required to be performed by a large number of players in, more or less, unison. Subsequently, in the issue 9 version, all these "challenges" remained identical in form but became much less individual in orientation. The old version of the Hamidon encounter allowed players to work together (and, yes, sometimes apart and at odds) to achieve a common goal *while maintaining a sense of self.* The new version forced players to relinquish that same sense of self in order to defeat the Hamidon. Attendance, enjoyment, and the anti-aesthetic of play all suffered as a result.

Admittedly, however, in *CoH/V*—and, indeed, in all MMOs, because of the complexity of their code and their play—there are some doubts as to whether forcing *CoH/V* players to obey social play restrictions ruined the pleasures of the original *CoH/V* Hamidon encounter. At about the same time, for instance, the Hamidon loot was drastically devalued. And the Hamidon encounter had been around for some time by May 2007, rendering it increasingly less novel for advanced *CoH/V* players. So, although the ruination of the Hamidon encounter is fairly well documented, and although that ruination can be reasonably attributed to a failure of the game design to adhere to an individually oriented anti-aesthetic of play, that ruination might reasonably be attributed to other factors as well.

In the next chapter, I (actually, Twixt) put these accusations of a predictable and repressive function of structured social play to more thorough scrutiny and analysis. What happens, for instance, when the social rules supporting group play and the game code supporting individual play are in conflict? In such a circumstance, do game players prefer the play of the social, or do they prefer instead the rules of the game? Who wins and who loses (and who has the most fun) when social interaction and individual play are at odds?

CHAPTER 11

Play and Punishment

I do not like thee, Doctor Fell.

—Thomas Brown, extempore (ca. 1680)

In 1967, Harold Garfinkel published *Studies in Ethnomethodology*, in which he presented and popularized "Garfinkeling" as a means of documenting the methods by which individuals create and sustain social order. Professor Garfinkel and his students performed a series of "breaching experiments" in which conventional social orders were interrupted; the consequences of those breachings were then examined in order to investigate the mechanisms by which social order was reconstituted.

The goal of the original Garfinkeling studies was to investigate assumptions in prevailing sociological theory—for example, functionalism[1]—that maintained social groups operated according to universal laws and norms. These laws were based on, by and large, individual and rational decision making.[2]

In contrast, Garfinkel found social decision making more immediate, interactive, and, importantly, fragile in its constitution and adoption of social rules. These social rules were then "rational" only to the extent that they were subsequently examined in the context of scientific inquiry.

> Scientific rationalities, in fact, occur as stable properties of actions and as sanctionable ideals only in the case of actions governed by the attitude of scientific theorizing. By contrast, actions governed by the attitude of daily life are marked by the specific absence of these rationalities either as stable properties or as sanctionable ideals.[3]

The branch of sociology that Garfinkel came to be associated with, ethnomethodology, was founded on this realization: that social law cannot be verified in any real or objective sense either by members of the social order or, equally important, by the scientists who attempt to study and confirm that social order. Professor Garfinkel concluded, in fact, that social order was not reconstituted with the aid of but, rather, *in the absence of* an objective social law. Subsequently, ethnomethodologists have found a great deal of diversity in social order, which is therein considered more indicative of social agency— or "contingency"—than rationality. And this assumption is now a basic tenet of cultural studies of computer games—particularly online MMOs.

Like Garfinkel some forty years ago, contemporary ethnomethodologies of MMOs have found a great deal of diversity in online social play. Yet in all the MMOs under scrutiny, there is a single and objective game code. And this game code, with the aid of an equally singular and objective game interface, establishes a common context for online play, without regard to subsequent intervention by either individuals or groups.

How, then, does social order function inside a virtual MMO, where law and order (*interface* and *code*) are more easily—and more objectively— verified than in the real-world settings of Garfinkel's original studies? What happens when social rules of convention come into conflict with game rules of code? During the latter part of 2007 and early 2008, playing Twixt inside *CoH/V*, I found out.

While Garfinkeling normally requires some sort of explicit social rules-breaking process, a similar Garfinkeling procedure might be accomplished within MMOs simply by adhering to the rules and spirit of the game—or the letter of the law, as it were—in those circumstances where MMO PvP game rules are verifiably distinct from the in-game social orders and etiquettes of more cooperative play.

TWIXT: THE RELUCTANT ETHNOMETHODOLOGIST

In the latter half of 2006, issue 7 of *CoH/V* introduced a dedicated PvP zone designed for battle among the game's most advanced characters (levels 40 to 50), with heroes opposing villains in attempting to capture six of seven "pillboxes."

Recluse's Victory (Levels 40–50, PvP, COV and COH)—Recluse's Victory represents the villains' assault on Paragon City™. Heroes and villains battle for control points, use heavy artillery to their advantage, and watch the zone change dynamically as a result of their efforts . . .

The main Goal of Recluse's Victory is to secure the Temporal Anchors, aka the pillboxes. Pillboxes are cross-shaped platforms with a central open-topped control area, with a turret on each of the 4 arms. In their neutral state, pillboxes boast a defense system of 4 boss ball turrets with amazing range, accuracy and firepower. In order to take over a pillbox all 4 turrets must be destroyed, which will enable the holographic control system to be clicked on. Once clicked on (a 5 second timer, interruptible) the temporal anchor will be set to your side, and the Pillbox and surroundings will change to either Hero or Villain under your feet. Remember that everyone knows what you just did, so expect company.[4]

At the time Recluse's Victory (RV) was introduced, my primary character, Twixt—a superhero "scrapper" in the game's archetypal scheme—was well known and well situated within the CoH/V community. After RV and other PvP components were introduced to CoH/V, it became increasingly evident that these newly competitive play elements opposed and, in the opposition, revealed the game's cooperative play norms. In a sense, by introducing PvP competition, the designers of CoH/V had Garfinkeled their game. I further explored this with Twixt.

Whenever Twixt was inside the RV zone, he played to win the zone—that is, Twixt abided entirely by the objective rules of the PvP game, as set forth and confirmed by the CoH/V game developers and moderators, without reference to or concern with any social rules of conduct established by CoH/V players outside the PvP game context.[5] At first, my interest was solely in adapting and perfecting Twixt's play to accomplish the PvP game goals. I did not expect anything like the severity—or the ferocity—of what occurred as a result.

GARFINKELING IN *CoH/V*

Player populations in CoH/V are divided across eleven U.S. servers, with a roughly equal number of players on each. Twixt originally played on the Champion server, one of several U.S. West Coast servers, with a mid-range population of players. After observing reactions to Twixt's behavior in RV on the Champion server over the course of several months, I created a similar Twixt character on the Infinity server, with similar results. Finally, after NCsoft instituted inter-server character transfers in late 2007, I transferred

Twixt to the game's most populous U.S. East Coast server, Freedom, and again repeated Twixt's single-minded, win-the-zone-at-all-costs competitive play inside Recluse's Victory. On each server, reactions to Twixt's play were strong, persistent over time, and, given small variations, extremely consistent.

While Twixt engaged in many activities inside RV that were deemed objectionable by portions of the *CoH/V* community, one in particular drew player wrath. The most notorious Twixt play involved teleport-related PvP tactics within RV: "droning" and, closely related, teleporting opponents into non-player characters (NPCs).

Since RV is a two-faction (heroes vs. villains) implementation of the game, there are safe areas within the RV zone where heroes and villains can enter and leave the zone without fear of being attacked. Protecting these safe areas ("bases") are security drones, which, without recourse, vaporize members of the opposing faction and transport them back to their own base on the opposite side of the zone map. There is no game-imposed penalty for getting droned, nor is any reward given to a player whose opponent gets droned.

Twixt—and all characters in *CoH/V*—have access to (should they choose it) a "teleport-foe" power, which allows the character to transport an opponent (within some limited range) next to them. If the teleporting character is standing by a group of friendly non-player characters and transports an opponent to that spot, then the opponent is attacked by the NPCs. If the teleporting character is standing by a drone and transports an opponent to that spot, then that opponent gets "droned" and vaporized.

According to player custom and according to a long series of discussions on the *CoH/V* public online forums, droning and teleporting into NPCs were forbidden. But from Twixt's oppositional point of view, droning and other sorts of aggressive teleporting were quite useful to delay or otherwise thwart villain intentions, particularly in cases where the villain contingent outnumbered hero players within the zone. Therefore, Twixt used the teleport-foe tactic whenever necessary and available; and this single tactic, though not the only effective characteristic of his play, came to be considered his most severe breach of etiquette.

As a result of his teleporting tactics, Twixt was often "petitioned" by opponents with the intention of having him banned from the game. The game's petition process offered a useful mechanism for determining what was and was not an enforceable rule of the game versus merely a player-imposed rule of conduct. Using obscene language in the game's broadcast channels, for instance, was clearly against the game's end-user license agreement (EULA) and was both a petitionable and actionable offense, regardless of any individual player's desires or preferences. Droning, on the other hand, was equally clearly an acceptable tactic, as determined by the game design and as confirmed by the lack of moderator intervention on any petitioner's behalf.

Nevertheless, droning remained widely (though not unanimously) denigrated as a "skill-less" tactic, ruining otherwise "fun" battles. In these valuations, one group of players (e.g., those without the teleport-foe power) were able to avoid being subject to (and thus having to defend against) the actions of another group of players, giving them significant competitive advantages within the zone. In fact, teleporting of all sorts decreased as a result of the negative social pressures exerted against droning. Twixt's particular set of powers (or "basic characteristics," in my earlier terms), which depended, in several different ways, on variations of the teleportation power, proved quite effective in RV yet remained heavily criticized and largely unused by other players.

While rigidly competitive PvP tactics[6] marked Twixt's play from the play of most others within RV, there were some other players who, after observing Twixt's success in the zone, copied his tactics and attitude.[7] But this copycat play normally had the support of some larger social group that also opposed, for various reasons, cooperative play in a competitive game context. Twixt was the only character observed through a yearlong period of play within RV who sustained his play without any accompanying social support.

CONSEQUENCES OF THE CODE

Prior to Twixt's competitive play in RV, his character had several, multi-year relationships with other *CoH/V* players; these relationships were, by and large, respectful, congenial, and enjoyable. Twixt had been invited and accepted into several supergroups during his career in the game, which waxed and waned with the coming and going of game players and game issues. At the time of Twixt's play in RV, his closest social affiliation was with members of a supergroup that was one of the higher rated (i.e., more accomplished) supergroups on the Champion server.

Initially, Twixt's success in disrupting villain activity in RV was admired, though somewhat begrudgingly, by his online friends and acquaintances, who, when circumstances permitted, fought villains alongside him. A factor that probably helped Twixt's early treatment in this regard was that as soon as his tactics became obvious, his actions became widely publicized on the game's public forums and, as a result, increasingly notorious. After trying and failing to convince Twixt to play "properly" in the broadcast channels available within RV, disgruntled players quickly took their pleas to the game's moderators (through petitions) and then, equally quickly, to the larger community of *CoH/V* players. As a result, Twixt became well known to friends and foes alike, and this minor level of celebrity was partially shared by those who associated with him.

The public messages that reacted negatively to Twixt's behavior during his initial period of play on each server were very similar. The following message, one of the more articulate (and less obscene), appeared soon after Twixt had moved to the Freedom server.[8]

> *Fri Jan 04 2008*
> ok seriously . . . where did this person come from. I know tp foe'ing into mobs is considered "legal" but this person is really getting out of hand. I can deal with his droning no problem, but now he's resorted to tp'ing into turrets and letting you get killed seriously . . . is there anything you can do about this particular individual. i mean it's pretty bad when his own faction hates him, but this guy has got to go.

As time went on and reprimands such as these had little effect, messages increasingly turned to various sorts of name-calling.

> *Sat Jan 05 2008*
> awww twixt, had a go at him teh other day in rv after i couldnt take my team bein tp foe'd into a drone anymore, we all agreed he is a n00b LOL

> *Sat Jan 05 2008*
> tp into mobs is a joke, into turrets can suck if your not ready, into heavies is game over, and into drones is just being a poor little loser.

Messages left in the game's synchronous, live chat channels were more direct and explicit.

01-12-2007 [*Broadcast*] twixt is a tool
✿

01-12-2007 [*Broadcast*] twixt is a jerk, get used to it
✿

01-12-2007 [*Broadcast*] twixt is a pussy lawl
✿

04-12-2007 [*Arena*] FYI twist is a fucking idiot

These messages promoted a rationale for Twixt's play in which he was either too ignorant ("retarded"), too young (a "noob"), or too mean (a "griefer") to understand or obey the social norms of cooperative play. Occasionally—but only occasionally—Twixt's play elicited support from other players or, equally infrequently, consideration of the broader game context that allowed Twixt's play to be, in the context of the PvP game inside RV, very successful.

12-13-2007 [*Broadcast*] I like twixt
12-13-2007 [*Broadcast*] lol
12-13-2007 [*Broadcast*] no i do its funny how he pisses all of u off
✿

01-09-2008 [*Broadcast*] . . . honestly twist is an obvi skilled player he just uses his skills in the wrong way lol

Thu Aug 09 2007
People dont like the way Twixt pvp's, some, including me thinks he is cowardly in his style. However, why make a big deal about someone doing something in a zone that is specifically designed for players to defeat other players?

One of the more common and consistent characterizations of Twixt involved denigrating his success within the zone as being accomplished without "skill."

05-06-2007 [*Broadcast*] YA he has to make up for the lack of skill with cheep tackics
✿

05-06-2007 [*Broadcast*] youhavtea to be lowest skilled pvper in game
✿

05-06-2007 [*Broadcast*] you have no skill
✿

12-23-2007 [*Broadcast*] you have no build, just tpfoe, nem staff, and lazer beam eyes

The inability of Twixt's opponents to acknowledge his success in zone play was no doubt motivated in some part by having entirely different, more socially oriented game goals. However, the degree to which villain messages and in-game claims distorted and transformed Twixt's play was drastic. For instance, Twixt was able to win the zone (capture six pillboxes for the heroes) literally hundreds of times during his yearlong period of play on three different servers. Twixt's opponents during this same period may have won the zone, in total, less than twenty times. Twixt was normally able to defeat, on average, ten to twenty villains a night, while villains seldom defeated ("killed") him more than once or twice during the same period of play—or, more often, didn't kill him at all.

Rather than acknowledge these successes, Twixt's opponents refused to admit them. Whenever Twixt pointed to the objective results of his play, he was ridiculed and ignored. At one point, for instance, toward the end of play on the Freedom server, Twixt posted verbatim transcripts of the game's online combat log as a confirming account of what had occurred during RV play. This posting drew severe criticism—most harshly from those players listed in the log as defeated by Twixt: several denied their defeats outright; others attributed their defeats to more devious or pitiable causes (including a rather long and detailed post drawing parallels between Twixt's behavior and Asperger's syndrome).

Much of this critical reaction to Twixt's play can be considered a sort of play itself. And, indeed, most of the responses to Twixt's play can be interpreted as a form of trash talk, common in competitive sports. However, there were several incidents that forced a re-evaluation of the context and the seriousness of player reactions to Twixt. The first of these was the rather sudden and unexpected expulsion of Twixt from his Champion-based supergroup.

The event that marked the beginning of Twixt's forced isolation from the Champion community occurred about three months after Twixt had begun using competitive tactics inside RV. After droning one of the more respected members of his supergroup (playing as a villain), Twixt received this curt, private communication from the group's leader:

03-21-2007 22:32:25 [*Tell*] you're banned you really pissed him off
03-21-2007 22:33:05 [*Tell*] Twixt —> hoho, sorry
03-21-2007 22:35:43 [*Tell*] yea real bad too twixt, he doens't care about the mob or the debt the drones is bs

And that was it. The subsequent lack of reconciliation from any of Twixt's previous longtime acquaintances within the supergroup seemed to indicate a culmination of that group's increasingly hostile and previously repressed feelings toward Twixt and his play.

There were also—during Twixt's early play in RV—some messages with more serious tones and emphases.

10-09-2006 [*Broadcast*] leave me alone you FUCKING CUNT

10-09-2006 [*Broadcast*] i swear if i ever meet you i will physically kill you for real

Throughout the duration of his competitive play inside Recluse's Victory, Twixt endured threats of computer sabotage, real-life violence, and a variety of less speculative (and more achievable) in-game harassments and abuses. This pattern of escalating feelings and emotions was repeated very similarly on each of the three servers Twixt visited. Because of the intensity of these private messages and because of his opponents' frequent supra-game tactics of unmercifully spamming Twixt's private message channels, it was often necessary for Twixt to turn off the game's communications functions entirely. This then effectively prevented me, as a player, from re-establishing social communications with other players, whether or not I wished to do so.

During the period in which Twixt moved from the Champion server to the Infinity server and, eventually, to the Freedom server, his notoriety as a player increased, and the negative reactions to his play were increasingly justified and reinforced through stereotypical (and false) characterizations of that play. These characterizations were repeated in lengthy public forum discussions in which Twixt as a game player—and as a person—was denigrated and marginalized.

Surprisingly, considering Twixt's single-minded behavior within RV, few of these discussions, whether in public or private, acknowledged Twixt's allegiance to the rules of the PvP game. In the beginning, Twixt played by these rules largely in silence; as time went by, I became increasingly verbal in an attempt to explain Twixt's goals and motivations. Without exception, however, the rules of the game, while not alien to Twixt's opponents, were deemed irrelevant in judging Twixt's play.

05-28-2007 [*Broadcast*] **Twixt:** so why ignore the rules of the game

05-28-2007 [*Broadcast*] Get your head out of your ass

05-28-2007 [*Broadcast*] There are no rules Twixt

○

02-24-2008 [*Broadcast*] **Twixt:** well, actually, i have been quite verbal here on freedom attempting to explain . . .

02-24-2008 [*Broadcast*] we don't care

02-24-2008 [*Broadcast*] stfu

One of the least confrontational and, correspondingly, most informative messages summarizing the attitudes other players adopted toward Twixt's play was this one, submitted late in Twixt's career:

Thu Mar 06 2008

. . . Twixt seems totally unable to comprehend other players as real people, and plays his own solipsistic game deliberately making others miserable.

. . . From his posts and RV broadcasts/actions, it's very clear that there really is something wrong with him that shouldn't be made fun of or laughed about. He writes in the exact same way as my paranoid schizophrenic uncle, going on and on about everything solely from his point of view, as if he is talking to himself while peppering his paragraphs with consistent typos and unecessarily long words.

His motive has remained unchanged ever since Issue 7—he plays this game because he believes it is his sole (and very serious) responsibility to maintain Hero supremacy in RV. He fights to win the zone and ruin every villains' day. It's almost like he's an NPC, and if you consider him in that light everything makes a lot more sense.

I truly believe he simply does not understand the feelings that lay behind people shouting and screaming at him in RV, and just continues to soldier on with his mission, wondering why the other Heroes aren't helping him rid RV of the bad guys with a sincerity that can almost make you sympathise with him.

Eventually, because of the recalcitrance of Twixt's opponents, it became increasingly difficult to interpret the social rules, orders, and behaviors associated with cooperative play—particularly cooperative play apart from and in opposition to any attempt to achieve PvP game goals—as anything other than a means of repressing individual play and players such as Twixt. From Twixt's point of view, playing by the rules of the game, winning the RV zone competitions, only increased the obstacles he faced and the insults he received. In fact, after Twixt had become sufficiently well known, the consensual goal within RV was, for extended periods of play, simply to "kill" Twixt.

02-24-2007 [*Broadcast*] before i di ei jsut wanna kill twixt atleast once
✿

03-21-2007 [*Broadcast*] Kill twixt for me please
✿

05-26-2007 [*Broadcast*] Kill Twixt once for me, dudesl. I'd have helped you but . . . well, you know.

☼

11-19-2007 [*Broadcast*] any other heros want confuse>? to kill twixt lol
☼

02-23-2008 [*Broadcast*] u guys shld kill twixt
☼

02-03-2008 [*Broadcast*] kill twixt for me!
☼

03-02-2008 [*Broadcast*] please do kill Twixt

Established player groups within RV were also quick to communicate their opinions of Twixt to other players. These communications bordered on coercion, applying the same tactics against potential Twixt allies as against Twixt himself: ridicule and the threat (or actuality) of social ostracism.

04-29-2007 [*Broadcast*] why you helping twixt for by the way ?
☼

06-15-2007 [*Broadcast*] lol someone actually helping twixt
☼

08-14-2007 [*Broadcast*] i hope you aren't helping twixt
08-14-2007 [*Broadcast*] nope . . . im not

These social pressures had strong effects on competitive play within RV. Players who played similarly to Twixt (e.g., those who made frequent use of the teleportation power) became subject to the same harsh treatment as Twixt. As a result, these players either altered their behavior or left RV entirely. This diminished the number and variety of characters and strategies players used within RV and, correspondingly, diminished the opportunity and likelihood of either new toons or tactics emerging to challenge those of the zone's more dominant and vocal players.

SOCIAL PLAY AND REPRESSION

There is a great deal of literature on the nature and treatment of deviant behavior (Goode 2008). Equally relevant here, however, are those studies in cultural psychology noting similarities among how members of a dominant culture represent non-members. These representations use precisely the same tactics—predominantly inferences of inferiority (immaturity, ignorance)—that were used in *CoH/V* to label and typecast Twixt. A well-known example in this regard (as noted in Cole 1996) are those characteristics nineteenth-century Europeans attached to the native cultures of their foreign conquests: for example, "an inability to control the emotions, animistic thinking, [and an] inability to reason out cause or plan for the future."[9]

Lending some potential credibility to these characterizations has been the ambiguity of the relationship between claims of a particular culture's superiority (by members of that culture) and the "evidence" used to validate those claims. That is, success on the battlefield or in the marketplace (or, equally, in a game) might depend on a great number of variables, many beyond human control and understanding. Nevertheless, these isolated and random outcomes are then taken as indications of a particular culture's intellectual or moral superiority—without any accompanying or subsequent tests of verification. Admittedly, such tests would, under normal conditions, be difficult, if not impossible, to conduct, let alone replicate. However, it is largely for this reason—the inability to verify claims of one culture in opposition to those of some other culture—that social constructivists have recommended abandoning the more essentialist assumptions of functionalism and instead focusing on those methodologies by which individuals come to accept or reject their otherwise empirically arbitrary and objectively indeterminable social status (e.g., labeling theory).[10]

Similarly, many studies of deviant behavior have assumed that the same social structures that react to and condemn deviant behaviors are those structures in which those behaviors originate and are best understood. These, too, are fundamentally constructivist assumptions implying a relative notion of deviance, in which deviant behavior is not necessarily a violation of anything absolute or essential.

Within *CoH/V* and other similar, socially oriented role-playing games, however, there are embedded rules for game play and in-game behavior determined entirely by the game code and interface; these rules exist prior to and apart from the many, varied, and sometimes contradictory social rules that later emerge among players. Twixt's behavior within RV, for instance, was purposefully governed and guided by the rules of the RV game; and most players' negative and critical reactions to Twixt's play were peripheral to and, in many cases, contrary to those same rules. In this sense—that is, in the reification of game rules as "natural" laws—Twixt's play was non-deviant, conforming to an absolute and essential set of values. In a similar sense, negative and critical reactions to Twixt's play can be seen as non-conforming and "deviant" in prioritizing a limited set of players' interests and concerns.

Garfinkel's original breaching experiments—and more-recent ethnomethodological accounts of online societies[11]—have often focused on how individuals in unfamiliar social contexts learn, negotiate, or are taught prevailing social norms; they have focused less often on what those social norms actually are. In the context of *CoH/V*, since Twixt's competitive play referenced explicit game rules as set forth by the game designers, there is a relative lack of ambiguity in making this determination.

In real-world environments, "natural" laws governing social relationships, if they exist at all, are part of the same social system in which they operate and, for that reason, are difficult to isolate, measure, and confirm. In Twixt's case, however, two unique sets of rules—one governing the game system, one governing the game "society"—offered an opportunity to observe how social rules adapt to system rules (or, more speculatively, how social laws might *reproduce* natural laws). And the clearest answer, based on Twixt's experience, is that they don't. Rather, if game rules suddenly pose some threat to existing social order, those game rules are simply ignored. And further, if some player—like Twixt—decides to explore those rules fully, then that player is shunned, silenced, and, if at all possible, expelled.

As a simulation of real-world society, virtual societies within online games suffer due to the bound and predetermined nature of their system rules. However, as a platform for investigating the degree to which social orders are capable of revealing and unraveling broader system rules, online games such as *CoH/V* indicate that socially oriented and strictly cooperative group play, as a whole, is much more repressive and much less capable of exploring system potentials than is individual, idiosyncratic, oppositional, and competitive play.[12]

Indeed, the strong, negative, and emotional reactions to Twixt's play were almost always focused on preserving beneficent social communities and friendships in blatant disregard of game rules. The most important negative consequence of Twixt's behavior in the eyes of other players, then, was not his failure to achieve game goals—Twixt's opponents "failed" this test more often than he did—but his failure to garner and sustain social connections: the most repellant consequence of Twixt playing to win was that it made him *disliked*.

04-12-2007 [*Broadcast*] Everybody hates Twixt, huh?

✿

12-23-2007 [*Broadcast*] yea he is hated by a few servers . . .

✿

01-22-2008 [*Broadcast*] just proves how much everyone hates twixt =D

◆

02-15-2008 [*Broadcast*] you know, the guy even the heroes hate

◆

03-15-2008 [*Broadcast*] Twixt be quiet, every villain i know hates u even tho im a hero

Remaining likable—socially connected—within the *CoH/V* community meant playing the game according to values other than those made explicit by code and interface. Players could only learn these values—much like those affecting social activities in the real world—by becoming (or already being) a member of the game's entrenched social order.

THE LESSONS OF TWIXT

The most surprising result of Twixt's play within RV was not merely the severity of the negative reactions to his play, but the degree to which game rules played such an insignificant role in those reactions. That is, a significant part of the social order within *CoH/V* seemed to operate quite independently of game rules and almost solely for the sake of its own preservation. It did not seem within the purview of social orders and ordering within *CoH/V* to recognize (much less nurture) any sort of rationality—or, for that matter, any other supra-social mechanism that might have adjudicated Twixt's play on the basis of its ability to provide, over time, greater knowledge of the game system or, in a broader sense, what Sutton-Smith (2001) calls "the potentiation of adaptive variability."[13]

The *CoH/V* online society had a decidedly chilling effect on this variability function. Given the adaptive value of individual play in exploring and revealing system characteristics, the social pressures against this sort of play in *CoH/V* seem drastically and overly harsh, even unnatural. If either natural or system laws governing social order in the real world are in any way analogous to the game rules of the *CoH/V* virtual world, we might conclude that social orders in general are more likely to deny than reveal these laws. It is only through so-called aberrations or "deviant" behavior—in Twixt's case, through what might be regarded as "breaching" (or "bad") play—that system rules, mechanics, and laws can be made most evident and applied most indiscriminately within a cooperative and self-sustaining social order.

CHAPTER 12

Final Comments

It's-a-me!
—Mario

Computer game play employs an *anti* or oppositional cognitive function that, in its recursive application, forms contexts of values within which subsequent play, subsequent opposition, subsequent contextualization, and subsequent valuation take place. Computer game play is most fundamentally an individual activity. This individual activity may—and frequently does—occur in social contexts, but in those social contexts, individual play is typically restricted and repressed in order to conform to and sustain social order. Further, the cognitive functions of play are universal and common in form; these formal properties of play are then closely related to the manipulation of signs and symbols in other contexts: human *semiosis*.

If we assume that opposition, contextualization, and recursion are, in their general application, common within computer game design and structure, and if we further assume that these functions are indicative of analogous functions in human cognition, then we can, without detailing the precise biological mechanisms of these functions, make some general comments concerning the consequences of their application during computer game play.

Computer games are meaning-making machines that, during repeated and recursive play, devalue real-world values of signs and symbols and, during that process, substitute values more relevant to the structure of the game system and, most particularly, more relevant to the identification and construction of the most desired game objects. Simulations intended to model the real world do so by creating game signs and symbols that have similar uses—and, thus, similar values—to their real-world referents. But games and game play are not, in most cases, either most appealing or most success-ful when game object values are determined, as they are in simulations, by something other than the process of play itself.

Human players appear most comfortable and most proficient during play with game systems homologous to human cognitive architectures. These innate architectures are not always consistent with the real-world environments in which they have evolved. The real world, for instance, is almost certainly more complex than human cognition assumes. Correspondingly, game designs are, in general, more likely to reflect a level of structural complexity more compatible with human sensibilities than with a more objectively realized natural world.

Yet, despite game designs being practically bound by some upper limit of human cognition, the play process is quite capable of generating, within these bounds, a large variety of values and meanings. Through successive contextualizations—recontextualization and supra-contextualization—these values and meanings can extend beyond their in-game uses and, in some cases, challenge and replace real-world values and meanings. This potential is increasingly likely when the real-world values of signs and symbols are mediated by the same technological interfaces and affordances as those found within computer games.

Human cognitive architectures require an embodiment of form. Likewise, computer games require an embodiment of play. Computer games are conventionally accessed through a ubiquitous controller, which requires the habituation of player response. This habituation process embodies the computer game aesthetic experience prior to player engagement with those semiotic properties (the values and meanings of game objects) that subsequently emerge during play.

The habituation required by computer games is at least partially in parallel with the tenets of a formalist model of literature in which "literariness" is assigned a fundamentally dehabituation function. Through the dehabituation function of poetic language, the conventions—the illusions—of natural language are revealed and, in that realization, reference a more immediate, pre-linguistic experience.

Yet, while natural language and the mechanical necessities of computer game play (its *interface*) evoke similar habituations, computer game play has no parallel to the dehabituation function of poetic language. On the contrary, computer game play, because it is accessed solely through its own physical mechanic, tends to embody and affirm its own conventions and illusions. Therein, the aesthetic experience of the computer game becomes a self-referencing and self-contained meaning-making process that cannot easily (if at all) stand in opposition, as poetic language can, to some other, preexisting experiential mode.

All language, including poetic language, is ultimately grounded in T. S. Eliot's notion of an "objective correlative," which situates that language within an intractable external reality. Computer game play, however, functions not in opposition to its real-world referents and values but in substitution for them. Computer game structures reflect our natural senses and those cognitive properties that interpret and value the natural senses, and this reflection is, once engaged, trapped within its embodiment. During computer game play, the narcissistic reflection of self becomes our source of aesthetic pleasure and the root of our subsequent seduction; and therein, for better or worse, computer game play becomes a visceral confirmation of the virtual.

In the closed system of fictional worlds, we are familiar with the willing suspension of disbelief. In the closed system of virtual worlds, that suspension of disbelief is replaced by active reinforcement of false experience, resulting in little to no distinction between what players want and what players believe. This is not a novel notion in new media aesthetics. Neil Postman (1986) calls this phenomenon "amusing ourselves to death"; Jean Baudrillaud (1988) describes it as an endless precession of simulacra, an age of the hyper-real, wherein there is no longer any necessity to reference a natural world; Katherine Hayles (1999) speaks of new media "disembodiment" and a "cyborg ideology"; and so forth.

The peculiar and self-aggrandizing *anti-aesthetic* of the computer game becomes very apparent in how natural laws fare when placed in opposition to game rules. During computer game play, virtually without exception, the natural laws of physics are ignored and reconstituted to better suit the laws of the psychophysical: the perceptions and expectations of game players.

This is evident in the distortion of the laws of gravity and momentum in arcade games—including *Spacewar,* one of the earliest video game designs.[1] Likewise, natural laws of probability are transformed to more appealingly reflect individual player sensibilities. This can be observed in the implementation of "hot-hand" algorithms in sports games—including the overly influential variable of a football team's "form" in *Football Manager* (Sports Interactive), *Hattrick* (Hattrick Ltd.), and elsewhere—and in the *CoH/V* "streak-breaker" code, which conforms to widely held but nevertheless incorrect human assumptions about the nature and distribution of random sequences.

The streak-breaker code breaks only miss streaks, and it breaks them for both heroes and villains. Who wants to have their hit streak broken?[2]

That is, if either a *CoH/V* hero or villain misses striking an NPC opponent more often than human perception deems feasible or proper, then that miss streak is broken by the *CoH/V* game code. The hero or villain is given an automatic hit, which, over time and many heroes and many villains, results in an improbable change in the natural laws of probability. These new and revised *psychophysical* laws of probability then affect player experiences with and expectations concerning the natural laws of probability. What is a genuine anomaly between human perception of random sequences and the reality of random sequences becomes a more fun and easy-to-get-along-with confirmation of human expectations of random sequences within the computer game.

Fortunately, in the natural world, the playful affirmation of the psychophysical is both a source of self-centered pleasure and, ultimately, a source of abrupt self-realization. Real-world laws, even when distorted by game rules, remain objectively demonstrable outside the game context, just as game rules remain objectively demonstrable through reference to game code. These and similar realities firmly establish a set of boundaries for computer game play and insure, upon repetitive and recursive play, that play is a parasitic and, ultimately, self-destructive form. That is, during play, players become increasingly self-aware (through reference to the formal mechanics of self-awareness) and increasingly less subject to the engagements, immersions, and related pleasures of self-absorption. For this reason, computer game play commonly becomes, over time, increasingly revealed and, as a result, increasingly boring; and at the point of boredom, newer and more novel attractions—another computer game, perhaps—are required to sustain any ongoing (anti-)aesthetic of play. Or, at least, this is the most normal consequence of play in its most common state, where it is fated by nature to create, to destroy, and, ultimately, to fail.

Based on current trends in game design and game studies, however, I have some uncertainties and concerns regarding individual play in the relatively un-natural state of virtual worlds—within MMORPGs, for instance, where games might be governed and ordered by a society of players rather than by the biological mechanics of play. These concerns are located neither in human play nor in interactive media but, rather, in the potency of those social norms that guide play behavior without need or opportunity to reference the natural environment in which human play originated. We face, in other words, no danger from play—play has aided our species since time immemorial. We face danger only from that which might prevent play from breaking its own rules: the rules and regulations of social policies.

In most social contexts, free and destructive play remains associated with and, assumedly, restricted to the immature, the untrained, or the criminal—and no doubt such restrictions have well served the needs of society and those architects of social systems who construct and maintain that society. Within online virtual worlds, however, social order tends to isolate, prosecute, and, if possible, eliminate all griefing and hacking and other so-called miscreant behaviors. This social order, when applied within virtual worlds similar to the current crop of MMORPGs, has significant potential to put natural laws and forms of play at risk.

Prior to this point in human history and the advent of pervasive social media, regardless of any maverick policy or misguided law, regardless of all restrictions and boundaries, play has maintained the capacity to *break free*. Indeed, the value of play emphasized here—to reveal something other than what is already known—assumes that play provides not only a different perspective but a meta-perspective. This meta-perspective allows play to break free of what is imagined or expected or desired—even unto what is denied and feared and least of all desired.[3]

Thus, as an embodied property of the human species, free and open play has remained secure from the more local and temporary effects of social influence, subdued from time to time, yet incorrigible. However, as virtual worlds evolve toward increasingly realistic interfaces and operating systems—which they show every indication of doing—play within these worlds seems increasingly likely to avoid the often distasteful revelations of the natural world in favor of the more pleasant and uncontested confirmations of a culturally situated and properly socialized self. Should social policy dictate the code and interface of virtual worlds for social benefit, then individual play within those worlds would no longer have recourse to nature. Natural law in such circumstances becomes the socially controlled conventions of *interface* and *code*. Play might still break things within such a socially determined world, but it would no longer have the capacity, based on the unpredictable revelations of play within nature, to break *free*.

A virtual world that traps, regulates, and purposefully distorts the overtly selfish behavior of individuals—including, prominently, play—appears to be a well-built bottle for one of our most destructive and most useful genies. I would hesitate to trap that genie permanently inside.

NOTES

Introduction

1. Huizinga 1955, foreword.
2. Huizinga 1955, 141.
3. Jamesson 1998.
4. Sutton-Smith 2001, 223–24.
5. Sutton-Smith 2001, 231.
6. Myers 1999, 485.
7. Here, of course, we must assume that there is indeed a common, universal, and biologically determined human interpretive process and an accompanying "code." But this is an assumption implicit in the formalist approach I will offer, and, in my mind, it is an assumption necessary to claim basic and common functions of human language.
8. Searle 2002, 60.
9. Barkow, Cosmides, & Tooby 1992, 5.
10. Barkow, Cosmides, & Tooby 1992, 5.

Chapter 1

1. Verenikina, Harris, & Lysaght 2003, online.
2. I might further summarize these, but Sutton-Smith (2001) has already done so. See his description of "rhetorics of progress" in *The Ambiguity of Play.*
3. For instance, when I have had occasion to lecture on computer games to middle-school students (not that often), I am normally positioned inside a computer lab of some sort where I have ready access to computer game examples and displays. Almost invariably in these circumstances, there are severe restrictions on how and when students can use this computer lab to play games—including, in one case, a huge banner on the wall behind my lectern, stating clearly, in two-foot-tall block letters, "NO COMPUTER GAME PLAYING!!!"
4. See Sun & Lin 2005 for examples of individual pleasures gained during "white-eyed" computer game grief play.
5. See Schechner 1988, 2002.
6. Hawley 2002, 2003.
7. See the analysis in Pellis & Pellis 1998 and Pellis & Iwaniuk 1999.
8. Ernulf & Innala 1995.
9. This uncertainty of being unable to detach normative context from any meaningful definition of aggressive, risky, or otherwise pejoratively labeled play also arises in the controversies surrounding the study of the biology of animal aggression. See Blanchard, Hebert, & Blanchard 1999.

10. For instance, one of the better-known and most widely cited examples of bad play in a virtual environment is the Mr. Bungle virtual rape episode as it took place within *LamdaMOO* and was reported in Dibble 1993.

11. An example would be throwing the game against the wall, a sort of *supra-contextual* play. See chapter 9.

12. *WoW* Hunter Discussion Forum, February 5, 2005.

13. Poker, in particular, is frequently enlivened and extended through the common social convention of allowing "dealer's choice" of rules.

14. An example is private negotiations between *Monopoly* players involving exchange of real-world currencies.

15. Garfinkel 1967.

16. See Harnard 1990.

17. These two types of rules are compared in Klabbers & Van der Waals 1989.

18. See the description of the design of *Civilization* in *The Nature of Computer Games* (Myers 2003, 132–33).

19. Edgerton 1985; Geyer & van der Zouwen 1986; Maturana & Varela 1980, 1987.

20. Suber 1990, online.

21. The Serious Games Institute at Coventry University reports "Serious games are digital computer games with an educational purpose. Their current main areas of application are in the business and military sectors but there is also much interest in their use in the education sector, especially primary and secondary education" (http://www.coventry.ac.uk/researchnet/d/440). The interested reader may also wish to Google "persuasive games" for similar definitions and initiatives.

22. For example, see Spariosu 1989.

Chapter 2

1. See Smith 1984; Bekoff & Byers 1998.

2. Bateson 1972.

3. This concept is based largely on the discussion in Huizinga 1955.

4. Sutton-Smith 2001, 221.

5. The phenomenon of film as "anti-perception" may be most obvious in its correspondingly rare exceptions. There are, after all, some films—film "events"—intentionally displayed in sensory-rich environments. Cult films—such as *The Rocky Horror Picture Show* (1975)—are often shown repetitively to a mutually well-known and largely community-based audience. The sensory and socially rich experience of such a display is aesthetically closer to the experience of a computer game than to that of film in general. However, the effects of such a display are determined by its relationship and reference to the broader film domain. In a context somewhat parallel to that of poetic language, audience interaction and social presence within the theater dehabitualize film conventions and restore some of the original immediacy and effects of an unmediated perception.

6. Descartes, *Principles of Philosophy.*

7. Merrill 1995, 141.

8. Derrida 1988.

9. It is similar in this respect to Aristotle's *energeia.*

10. Turner 1990, 11–12.

11. Spariosu 1997, 38.

Chapter 3

1. Erlich 1981.
2. Wellek 1991.
3. See, for instance, Jakobson 1956.
4. Erlich 1981, 158–59.
5. This is in accord with Erlich's (1981) analysis. Cf. pp. 231–32.
6. Compare, for instance, the relationship between formalist criticism and cognitive science to the relationship between formal linguistics and cognitive linguistics.
7. See Laughlin & d'Aquili 1974.
8. Currently—much more so than in the 1920s of Russian formalism—there are increasing references to forms of human experience and related perceptual mechanics relevant to an understanding of a cognitive-based aesthetics. See, for instance, the discussion of cognitive film theory in chapter 6.
9. "Art as Technique" (1917).
10. Andersen 1990, 216.
11. Manovich 2001, 64.
12. Miall & Kuiken 1999, 121.
13. *Neuroaesthetics* (Skov & Vartanian 2008), for instance, has some very important and interesting affinities with this approach but remains somewhat peripheral to an *anti*-aesthetic. Neuroaesthetics has tended to focus on the immediacy of the senses and sensory impressions; thus, neuroaesthetics most often concerns how well—or how poorly—music (aural stimuli) and painting (visual stimuli) might correlate with basic human preferences and desires (e.g., Livingstone 2002). My focus here is more on the mechanics of cognition—most particularly, semiosis—than, strictly speaking, the mechanics of the senses. Just as particular sorts of aural and visual data may be preferred by human eyes and human ears due to those organs' natural historical predilections for that sort of data, so particular data connections and data processing structures may well be preferred by the human brains that receive, interpret, and, importantly, transform that sensory data into symbolic form. This latter process—rather than the former—is more directly my concern and more likely an attributive feature of the anti-aesthetic. Certainly, however, the neuroaesthetic and the anti-aesthetic are on the same side of the fence in opposition to the currently more common and widespread assumptions of cultural studies.
14. For instance, Jakobson's "phenomenological structuralism" (see Holenstein 1977) and Ricoeur's (1981) "phenomenological hermeneutics" combine the study of subjective reader/player experiences with a more formal and objective study of texts.

Chapter 4

1. Andersen 1990.
2. Aarseth 1997.
3. Aarseth does, of course, also note the important cognitive consequence of certain ergodic art/text designs: for example, aporia and epiphany. See Aarseth 1999.
4. See Seifert 2008 for a list.
5. Rafaeli & Sudweeks 1997, online.
6. Myers 2003.
7. The innovative Nintendo Wii controller is unique among current controller designs and is characteristic of occasional attempts to broaden the range of body movements used as game commands. Significantly, though, the physical motions

allowed by the Wii controller remain abstract and only superficially related to their real-world analogs. For instance, there are several Wii-based golf games in which a golf swing is simulated by an arm swing of the Wii. However, computer game players—particularly computer game players who are also golfers—quickly learn that the most telling characteristic of these two motions is their dissimilarity. All Wii controller motions—regardless of their reference outside the game system—must be learned in the context of their in-game idiosyncrasies and then, for most successful play, applied with those idiosyncrasies in mind.

8. And, of course, computer game controllers are produced en masse—another reason for their similar and generic design.

9. For instance, playing the well-known *Zelda* (Nintendo) series with and without a Wii controller yields very little difference—once both controller types have been equally mastered—in the overall *feel* of the game. Once controller mechanics are practiced and habitualized, they then rarely—except in cases of severe over- or under-complexities—color our evaluation of computer game aesthetics.

10. See the figure in Myers 2007, 227.

11. Myers 2003, 66.

12. In literary contexts, these functions of play may be considered "subtropes": for example, aporia and epiphany (Aarseth). However, more neutral terms—opposition and contextualization—perhaps better represent these intrinsically motivated, instinctively evoked, and essentially mechanical functions of play.

13. Lakoff & Johnson 1999.

14. See Gibson 1979.

15. For instance, game objects can be put into opposition during play at some relatively minute contextual level (e.g., comparing the relative effectiveness of placing multiple houses or a single hotel on Park Place in *Monopoly*), or these objects may be more broadly conceived, up to and including the game player herself (e.g., comparing *Monopoly* players at the end of the game to determine a "winner").

16. Casti 2004, online.

17. Again, see the description of play as "adaptive variability" in Sutton-Smith 2001, 221–25.

18. Compare the goals of the designers of the game *Foldit* (Bourzac), which is an attempt to harness the creative energies of a repetitive and largely intuitive play process, with little to no consequence attached to abortive and/or failed attempts to achieve the game's winning conditions.

19. The imposition of narrative is a restriction precisely of this sort.

20. Myers 2003, 136–46.

21. Kuhn 2007, online.

22. This is dealt with in some detail in Rojas 1996.

23. This scheme is outlined in Rogers et al. 2007.

24. For a more thorough discussion of the repressive effects of this social play phenomenon, see the discussion of Twixt in chapter 11.

Chapter 5

1. Grodal 2003, 148.

2. Or, as stated earlier (in chapter 1), the computer game is an experience simulator and, simultaneously, the experience being simulated.

3. Aarseth 1997, 181–82.

4. Gadamer 1986, 12.

Chapter 6

1. Bruner 1990.
2. Piaget 1954.
3. See studies in "narrative psychology" for the use of narrative within constructivist theory and related qualitative methodologies.
4. Labov 1997.
5. Bevir 2000; Labov & Waletzky 1967.
6. Jakobson 1956.
7. Aarseth 1997.
8. Compare, for instance, "transgressional" literature.
9. Montfort 2003.
10. Ryan 1992.
11. Aarseth 1997, 92.
12. Myers 2003.
13. As do the rules of tic-tac-toe and the hypothetical T3 discussed in chapter 2.
14. See again figures 1.1 and 1.2 in chapter 1.
15. Grodal 2000, 2003; King & Krzywinska 2002.
16. Manovich 2001; Bolter & Grusin 2000.
17. See, for instance, Walther 2004.
18. Anderson 1996; Tan 1996.
19. Rascaroli 2002, online.
20. Mitry 1998.
21. This would likewise explain the de-prioritization of narrative in pornographic films.
22. See Bordwell 2006.
23. Aarseth 1997.
24. This is the explanation by film critic Andy Klein (2001).
25. Aarseth 1997 (see especially chapter 1).
26. Eskelinen 2004.
27. There are several varieties of the "film as illusion" argument; all are distinguished by the assumption that human responses to filmed images are determined by the mechanics of human perception (and cognition). These "mechanics" may be supplemented and transformed by subsequent interpretations, but these Johnny-come-lately interpretations are then neither fundamental nor particularly informative regarding the basic aesthetic properties of film.
28. Tan 1996.
29. Anderson 1996.
30. See chapter 3.
31. This is similar to Gunning's (1986) notion of "cinema of attraction." However, Gunning's analysis focuses on the impact of specific (and fleeting) historical contexts. The notion here is that the appeal of spectacle originates within common discriminative functions of perception (and cognition).
32. Critics may rightfully point to order and structure in, for instance, commercial television—in sitcoms, dramas, and narratives. Yet the popular media audience is engaged with the *whole* of media—a kaleidoscope of sensations, a "blooming, buzzing confusion"—which is simultaneously similar and different, ordered and disordered. Our media viewing (and playing) experience is then bound only by when and by what we are engaged and by when and by what we are disengaged. This engagement remains a disjointed experience until, selfishly, we impose some structure upon it.

Chapter 7

1. Dictionary.com (2009), online.
2. Ward 1999, online.
3. Chick 2008, online.
4. Orland n.d., online.
5. Miyamoto 2003, online.
6. For example, *Doom* and *Super Mario Bros., Legend of Zelda.*
7. For example, *Zork, Neverwinter Nights,* and most current online games, such as *World of Warcraft.*
8. Myers 2003, 115–16.
9. Garriot 1999.
10. Garriot 1999, online.
11. See http://www.moongates.com/Media/4-Return_To_Virtue.ram.
12. Bartle 1999.
13. See, for instance, the stories, events, and lore information available within the Stratics *Ultima Online* Web site, http://uo.stratics.com/index.shtml.
14. For instance, splitting the game between the Felucca and Trammel facets to more clearly and definitively isolate *red* player-characters, or player killers (PK'ers), from *blue* player-characters (non-PKers).
15. Myers 1984.
16. This includes the heroic quest template obvious within *UO* but also the rebel-Empire divisions in *Star Wars Galaxies,* the race warfare in *Dark Age of Camelot,* and the Axis-Allies conflict in *World War II Online.*
17. Inspect, for instance, the *City of Heroes* backstory. See http://www.cityof heroes.com/gameinfo/paragon_city.html.
18. Bartle 1999.
19. *MOO* served as one of the inspirations for the similar, more contemporary *Galactic Civilizations* series, as well as its recent real-time counterpart *Sins of a Solar Empire.* An analysis of *MOO* equally applies to these and many other similar strategy games.
20. Emrich is a former writer/editor at *Computer Gaming World.*
21. Keefer 2002, online.
22. Hosely 2003, online.
23. See http://apolyton.net/moo3/.
24. Chick 2003, online.
25. Anonymous 2003, online.

Chapter 8

1. Myers 1992.
2. See Myers 1991.
3. Myers 2003, 131–36.
4. See Myers 2003, 132–34.
5. Reynolds 1996, 179.
6. Anonymous 2004, online.
7. Myers 1991, 343.
8. For example, Aarseth's (1999) notion of a cyclical process alternating between aporia and epiphany.
9. Well, actually, I could say—in formal parallel with tech-based theorists such

as McLuhan (1964), for instance—that play is an inclusive process motivated by the peculiar characteristics of the brain. The key difference, then, between tech-based and my own, more "brain-based" theory (see the following text) is that, in the latter case, the brain must be considered an "external factor" constraining itself—resulting in, among other things, the common paradoxes of cognitive play (see Myers 2003, 65–68). Subsequently, some might eliminate these paradoxes through a sleight-of-hand semantics, setting up a false dichotomy of brain and mind, or mind and consciousness, or consciousness and play. Rather, I think these paradoxes of cognition, as reproduced in cognitive play, should be acknowledged, accepted, and embraced.

10. Reynolds 1996, 181–82.

11. See van den Belt n.d., online.

12. For an interpretation regarding the lessons/stories as opportunities for edification, see Squire 2002.

13. As advocating ideological perspective peculiar to Western civilization, see the examples following.

14. Henthorne 2003, online.

15. Quoted in Chick 2001, online.

16. Squire 2002; Caviness 2002; Stephenson 1999.

17. See Myers 2003, 39–44.

18. Chick (2001) also makes this point.

19. Anonymous 2002, online.

20. Lammes 2003, 124.

21. Douglas 2002, online.

22. In fact, after assigning a positive in-game value to barbarians, many players of the earliest versions of *Civilization* used a save-and-reload strategy to invade the same goody hut over and over again until it produced its most valuable (otherwise randomly determined) goody—a strategy considered aberrant and curtailed in later game designs by having the game code determine the contents of all goody hut caches prior to a point where the game could be conveniently reloaded.

23. Poblocki 2002, online.

24. Koster 2003, online.

25. Poblocki 2002, online.

26. Eskelinen 2001, online.

27. Douglas 2002, online.

28. See note 8 in chapter 4.

29. See Bekoff & Byers 1998.

30. See Clarke 1994 for a more general argument against the inherent educational and enculturation potential of new media.

31. Carr 2008, 229.

Chapter 9

1. That is, opposition and recursive contextualization—see "The Computer Game Code" in chapter 4.

2. Myers 2003, 121.

3. Rheingold 2000; Taylor 2006.

4. In chapter 1, such notions are discussed in regard to the contrary notion of "bad" play.

5. Salazar 2005, online.

6. Palo Alto Research Center 2005, online.

7. *Ali Baba and the Forty Thieves* (Quality Software, 1981) displayed most of the basic characteristics of later and more expansive MMOs.

8. Lakoff & Johnson (1999, 2003), for instance, have located the foundations for common language acquisition within image schemata: "conceptual models of human perception and cognition [that] explain how different spatial relationships are used in language" (Rodriguez & Egenhofer 1997, 3). See also chapter 4 in the present study.

9. Huizinga 1955, 1.

10. Horning 2006, online.

11. See also figure 4.1 in chapter 4.

12. See the description of the computer game *anti-aesthetic* in chapter 5.

13. Spariosu 1989, 47.

14. Taylor 2006, 159.

15. Myerson 1999, available online at http://home.uchicago.edu/~rmyerson/research/jelnash.pdf.

16. Sent 2004.

17. Shleifer 2000.

18. Linaza 1984, 271, quoting Piaget 1932, 81–82.

19. "Permadeath" occurs when an MMO player-character is defeated ("dies") and, as a result of that defeat ("death"), is permanently removed from the game, with no possibility of resurrection or reuse.

Chapter 10

1. Emmert 2005, online.

2. See chapter 4.

3. Bruce 2007, online.

4. *CoH/V* aficionados will quickly recognize that these same characteristics—and a similar level of popularity—are also closely associated with supra-group play during the well-known power-leveling extravaganzas that took place during the original *CoH/V* "Winter Lord" events.

5. Bruce 2005.

6. So others have shown (Malone 1981) and I have previously verified (Myers 1990).

Chapter 11

1. For example, social action theory—see Parsons 1937.

2. See, for instance, the discussion of rational choice theory in Scott 2000.

3. Garfinkel 1967, 270.

4. Foss 2006, online.

5. Thus, Twixt's behavior only "breached" the social rules of players, not the game rules of designers. For other examples of somewhat similar "breaching" play in MMOs, compare Twixt's story to the saga of Adam Ant in the early days of *Ultima Online* (see http://www.game-master.net/pit/ubbthreads.php) and to the adventures of Fansy the Famous Bard in *EverQuest 2* (see http://www.notaddicted.com/fansythefamous.php).

6. See Myers 2008.

7. A similar player attitude is described in Sirlin 2006.

8. I've included three types of messages to document player reactions to Twixt's

behavior. Inside RV, all players—heroes and villains—are able to type text messages that all can see in the game's broadcast channels, and these messages are labeled as such. Also, within RV and elsewhere in the game, players can choose to send private messages to one another that can be read only by the sender and receiver. These messages are commonly called "tells" and are labeled as "[*Tell*]." The third type of message appearing in this discussion is taken from the game's online public forums (https://boards.cityofheroes.com/ubbthreads.php). Each of these messages is listed with the date it first appeared, e.g., "*Sat Jan 05 2008.*"

9. Cole 1996, 16.

10. See Becker 1963.

11. See Taylor 2006.

12. It may be that these social pressures are more effective in virtual contexts than in real-world contexts due to the relative inability of virtual contexts to impose tests of fitness. Natural environments tend to judge the functionality and efficacy of rules and orders through, ultimately, physical tests of survival; in online MMORPG communities, group and individual survival is determined less by in-game achievements per se than by the number and utility of social connections that allow players to circumvent in-game tests and, correspondingly, in-game rules.

13. Sutton-Smith 2001, 231.

Chapter 12

1. See Myers 2003.

2. This rhetorical question was posed within the *City of Heroes* message forums on August 17, 2004, by "Weirdbeard," one of the Cryptic Studios programmers.

3. Simultaneously, this meta-perspective gives play its signature paradoxical nature, with which play theorists have long labored.

REFERENCES

Aaron, D. 1985. Playing with apocalypse. *New York Times Magazine,* December 29, 22.

Aarseth, E. 1997. *Cybertext: Perspectives on ergodic literature.* Baltimore, MD: Johns Hopkins University Press.

Aarseth, E. 1999. Aporia and epiphany in *Doom* and *The Speaking Clock:* The temporality of ergodic art. In M.-L. Ryan, ed., *Cyberspace textuality: Computer technology and literary theory,* 31–41. Bloomington: Indiana University Press.

Andersen, P. B. 1990. *A theory of computer semiotics.* Cambridge: Cambridge University Press.

Anderson, J. D. 1996. *The reality of illusion: An ecological approach to cognitive film theory.* Carbondale: Southern Illinois University Press.

Anonymous. 2002. *ICS—Infinite City strategy aka "Chinese" strategy (msg from "kilane royalist").* February 25. Retrieved January 18, 2004, from Apolyton Civ3 Strategy Forum, http://apolyton.net/forums/showthread.php?postid=773259#post773259.

Anonymous. 2003. *(msg from "[SDO]Guardian").* March 26. Retrieved June 14, 2003, from Infogrames Forum, http://www.inacommunity.com/forums/showthread.php?s=&threadid=282159.

Anonymous. 2004. *Civilization dirty tricks (msg from "Gus Smedstad").* January 18. Retrieved March 1, 2004, from the Cheater's Guild, http://www.cheaters-guild.com/cheat-display.asp?category=DirtyTricks&GameName=Civilization.

Barkow, J. H., L. Cosmides, & J. Tooby, eds. 1992. *The adapted mind: Evolutionary psychology and the evolution of culture.* New York: Oxford University Press.

Bartle, R. 1999. *Hearts, clubs, diamonds, spades: Players who suit MUDs.* August 28. Retrieved January 1, 2009, from Richard A. Bartle, http://www. mud.co.uk/richard/hcds.htm.

Bateson, G. 1972. *Steps to an ecology of mind.* New York: Ballantine Books.

Baudrillard, J. 1988. *Selected writings.* M. Posner, ed. Palo Alto, CA: Stanford University Press.

Becker, H. S. 1963. *Outsiders: Studies in the sociology of deviance.* New York: Free Press.

Bekoff, M., & J. A. Byers, eds. 1998. *Animal play: Evolutionary, comparative, and ecological perspectives.* Cambridge: Cambridge University Press.

Bevir, M. 2000. Narrative as a form of explanation. *Disputatio* 9:17–18.

Blanchard, D. C., M. Hebert, & R. J. Blanchard. 1999. *Continuity vs. (political) correctness: Animal models and human aggression.* Retrieved January 1, 2009, from the *HFG Review,* http://www.hfg.org/hfg_review/3/blanchard-hebert.htm.

Bolter, J. D., & R. Grusin. 2000. *Remediation: Understanding new media.* Cambridge, MA: MIT Press.

Bordwell, D. 1989. *Making meaning: Inference and rhetoric in the interpretation of cinema.* Cambridge, MA: Harvard University Press.

Bordwell, D. 2006. *The way Hollywood tells it: Story and style in modern movies.* Berkeley: University of California Press.

Bruce, C. 2005. *Redesigning the "Hamidon."* Retrieved August 1, 2009, from Issue 9 Breakthrough. http://www.cityofheroes.com/news/game_updates/issue_9/issue_9_breakthrough_redesigni.html.

Bruce, C. 2007. *Redesigning the "Hamidon."* Retrieved January 1, 2009, from *City of Heroes* Game Updates, http://www.cityofheroes.com/news/game_updates/issue_9/issue_9_breakthrough_redesigni.html.

Bruner, J. 1990. *Acts of meaning.* Cambridge, MA: Harvard University Press.

Caillois, R. 1961. *Man, play, and games.* New York: Free Press.

Carr, D. 2008. The trouble with *Civilization.* In B. Atkins & T. Krzyminksa, eds., *Videogame, Player, Text,* 222–35. Manchester, England: Manchester University Press.

Casti, J. L. 2004. *Synthetic thought.* February 19. Retrieved January 1, 2009, from *Nature,* http://www.nature.com/nature/journal/v427/n6976/full/427680a.html.

Caviness, R. 2002. *History in review:* Civilization III. May 14. Retrieved January 1, 2009, from History in Review, http://www.historyinreview.org/civiii.html.

Chick, T. 2001. *The fathers of* Civilization: *An interview with Sid Meier and Bruce Shelley.* August. Retrieved January 18, 2004, from CGOnline.com, http://www.cgonline.com/features/010829-i1-f1-pg5.html.

Chick, T. 2003. *60 minute review of* Master of Orion 3. February 21. Retrieved January 1, 2009, from Quarter to Three, http://www.quartertothree.com/reviews/moo3/moo3-1.shtml.

Chick, T. 2008. Metal Gear Solid 4: Guns of the Patriots *(PS3).* June 16. Retrieved January 1, 2009, from Crispy Gamer, http://www.crispygamer.com/gamereviews/2008-06-16/metal-gear-solid-4-guns-of-the-patriots-ps3.aspx.

Clarke, R. 1994. Media will never influence learning. *Educational Technology Research and Development* 42 (2): 21–29.

Cole, M. 1996. *Cultural psychology: A once and future discipline.* Cambridge, MA: Harvard University Press.

Copier, M. 2005. *Connecting worlds: Fantasy role-playing games, ritual acts, and the magic circle.* Retrieved January 1, 2009, from DiGRA 2005, Changing Views: Worlds in Play. http://www.digra.org/dl/db/06278.50594.pdf.

Csikszentmihalyi, M. 1991. *Flow: The psychology of optimal experience.* New York: Harper Perennial.

Derrida, J. 1988. Letter to a Japanese friend. In D. Wood & R. Bernasconi, eds., *Derrida and difference,* 1–5. Evanston, IL: Northwestern University Press.

Dibble, J. 1993. A rape in cyberspace. *Village Voice,* December 23, 36–42.

Douglas, C. 2002. *"You have unleashed a horde of barbarians": Fighting Indians, playing games, forming disciplines.* September. Retrieved January 1, 2009, from *Postmodern Culture,* http://www.iath.virginia.edu/pmc/text-only/issue.902/13.1douglas.txt.

Edgerton, R. B. 1985. *Rules, exceptions, and social order.* Berkeley: University of California Press.

Emmert, J. 2005. #2070950. January 14. Retrieved January 14, 2005, from *City of Heroes* Forums.

Erlich, V. 1981. *Russian formalism.* New Haven, CT: Yale University Press.

Ernulf, K., & S. Innala. 1995. Sexual bondage: A review and unobtrusive investigation. *Archives of Sexual Behavior* 24 (6): 631–54.

Eskelinen, M. 2001. The gaming situation. *Game Studies* 1 (1), http://gamestudies.org/0101/eskelinen/.

Eskelinen, M. 2004. *Six problems in search of a solution: The challenge of cybertext theory and ludology to literary theory.* Retrieved January 1, 2009, from *dichtung-digital,* http://www.brown.edu/Research/dichtung-digital/2004/3/Eskelinen/index.htm.

Foss, T. 2006. *Tips and strategems: Recluse's Victory.* Retrieved January 1, 2009, from *City of Heroes* Game Info: Official Guides, http://www.cityofheroes.com/game_info/official_guides/tips_and_stratagems_recluses_v.html.

Gadamer, H.-G. 1986. *The relevance of the beautiful, and other essays.* Cambridge: Cambridge University Press.

Garfinkel, H. 1967. *Studies in ethnomethodology.* Englewood Cliffs, NJ: Prentice-Hall.

Garriott, R. 1999. *An audience with Lord British.* November. Retrieved from Moongates.com, http://www.moongates.com/Articles/LordBritish_U9.htm.

Gee, J. P. 2003. *What video games have to teach us about learning and literacy.* New York: Palgrave Macmillan.

Geyer, F., & J. van der Zouwen, eds. 1986. *Sociocybernetic paradoxes: Observation, evolution, and control of self-steering systems.* London: Sage.

Gibson, J. 1979. *The ecological approach to visual perception.* Boston: Houghton Mifflin.

Goode, E. 2008. *Deviant Behavior,* 8th ed. New Jersey: Prentice Hall.

Grodal, T. 2000. Video games and the pleasures of control. In D. Zillmann & P. Vorderer, eds., *Media entertainment,* 197–214. Mahwah, NJ: Lawrence Erlbaum Associates.

Grodal, T. 2003. Stories for the eye, ear, and muscles: Video games, media, and embodied experience. In M. J. Wolf & B. Perron, eds., *The video game theory reader,* 129–56. New York: Routledge.

Gunning, T. 1986. The cinema of attractions: Early film, its spectators, and the avant-garde. *Wide Angle* 8 (3–4): 63–70.

Harnard, S. 1990. The symbol grounding problem. *Physica D* 42:335–46.

Hawley, P. H. 2002. Social dominance and prosocial and coercive strategies of resource control in preschoolers. *International Journal of Behavioral Development* 26:167–176.

Hawley, P. H. 2003. Prosocial and coercive configurations of resource control in early adolescence: The case for the well-adapted Machiavellian. *Merrill-Palmer Quarterly* 49 (3): 279–309.

Hayles, K. 1999. *How we became posthuman: Virtual bodies in cybernetics, literature, and informatics.* Chicago: University of Chicago Press.

Henthorne, T. 2003. *Cyber-utopias: The politics and ideology of computer games.* April. Retrieved January 1, 2009, from *Studies in Popular Culture,* http://www.pcasacas.org/SPC/spcissues/25.3/Henthorne.htm.

Holenstein, E. 1977. *Roman Jakobson's approach to language: Phenomenological structuralism.* Trans. C. Schelbert & T. Schelbert. Bloomington: Indiana University Press.

Horning, R. 2006. *Review of "Play between worlds: Exploring online game culture."* July 13. Retrieved January 1, 2009, from *Popmatters,* http://www.popmatters.com/pm/review/play-between-worlds/.

Hosely, R. 2003. *The art of* Master of Orion III. March 25. Retrieved from Macgamer, http://macgamer.com.

Huizinga, J. 1955. *Homo ludens: A study of the play-element in culture.* Boston: Beacon.

Jakobson, R. 1956. Two aspects of language and two types of aphasic disturbances. In R. Jakobson & M. Halle, eds., *Fundamentals of language,* 55–82. The Hague: Mouton.

Jakobson, R., & M. Halle, eds. 1956. *Fundamentals of language.* The Hague: Mouton.

Jamesson, F. 1998. *The cultural turn: Selected writings on the postmodern, 1983–1998.* New York: Verso.

Johnson-Laird, P. N. 1983. *Mental models: Towards a cognitive science of language, inference, and consciousness.* Cambridge, MA: Harvard University Press.

Keefer, J. 2002. Master of Orion 3: *High expectations.* June 27. Retrieved from Gamespy, http://www.gamespy.com/legacy/previews/moo3_a.shtm.

King, G., & T. Krzywinska, eds. 2002. *ScreenPlay: Cinema/videogames/interfaces.* London : Wallflower.

Kittler, F. A. 1997. *Gramophone, film, typewriter.* Trans. G. Geoffrey Winthrop-Young & M. Wurz. Stanford, CA: Stanford University Press.

Klabbers, J. 1996. Problem framing through gaming: Learning to manage complexity, uncertainty, and value adjustment. *Simulation & Gaming* 27:74–92.

Klabbers, J., & V. Van der Waals. 1989. From rigid-rule to free-form games: Observations on the role of rules. In J. Klabbers, W. Scheper, C. Takkenberg, & D. Crookall, eds., *Simulation-gaming: On the improvement of competence in dealing with complexity, uncertainty, and value conflicts,* 225–34. Oxford: Pergamon.

Klein, A. 2001. *Everything you wanted to know about "Memento."* Retrieved August 1, 2009, from salon.com.http://dir.salon.com/story/ent/movies/feature/2001/06/28/memento_analysis/print.html.

Koster, R. 2003. *A theory of fun.* September 11–13. Retrieved January 14, 2004, from Austin Games Conference, http://www.gameconference.com/conference/raphkoster.pdf.

Kuhn, S. 2007. *Prisoner's Dilemma.* Retrieved August 1, 2009, from Stanford Encyclopedia of Philosophy. http://plato.stanford.edu/entries/prisoner-dilemma/.

Labov, W. 1997. Retrieved January 1, 2009, from Some further steps in narrative analysis, http://www.ling.upenn.edu/~wlabov/sfs.html.

Labov, W., & J. Waletzky. 1967. Narrative analysis. In J. Helm, ed., *Essays on the verbal and visual arts,* 12–44. Seattle: University of Washington Press.

Lakoff, G., & M. Johnson. 1999. *Philosophy in the flesh: The embodied mind and its challenge to Western thought.* New York: Basic Books.

Lakoff, G., & M. Johnson. 2003. *Metaphors we live by.* Chicago: University of Chicago Press.

Lammes, S. 2003. On the border: The pleasure of exploration and colonial mastery in *Civilization III: Play the World.* In M. Copier & J. Raessens, eds., *Level up:*

Digital Games Research Conference proceedings, 120–29. Utrecht: University of Utrecht.

Laughlin, C. D., & E. G. d'Aquili. 1974. *Biogenetic structuralism*. New York: Columbia University Press.

Levi-Strauss, C. 1979. *Myth and meaning*. New York: Schocken Books.

Linaza, J. 1984. Piaget's marbles: The study of children's games and their knowledge of rules. *Oxford Review of Education* 10 (3): 271–74.

Livingstone, M. 2002. *Vision and art: The biology of seeing*. New York: Harry N. Abrams.

Malone, T. W. 1981. Toward a theory of intrinsically motivating instruction. *Cognitive Science* 4:333–69.

Manovich, L. 2001. *The language of new media*. Cambridge, MA: MIT Press.

Marr, D. 1982. *Vision: A computational investigation into the human representation and processing of visual information*. San Francisco: W. H. Freeman.

Maturana, H., & F. Varela. 1980. *Autopoiesis and cognition*. Dordrecht: D. Reidel.

Maturana, H., & F. Varela. 1987. *The tree of knowledge: The biological roots of human understanding*. Boston: New Science Library.

McLuhan, M. 1964. *Understanding media: The extensions of man*. New York: McGraw-Hill.

Merrill, F. 1995. *Semiosis in the post-modern age*. West Lafayette, IN: Purdue University Press.

Miall, D. S., & D. Kuiken. 1999. What is literariness? Three components of literary reading. *Discourse Processes* 28:121–38.

Mitry, J. 1998. *The aesthetics and psychology of the cinema*. Trans. C. King. London: Athlone.

Miyamoto, S. 2003. *Miyamoto interview:* SuperPLAY Magazine. April 23. Retrieved January 1, 2009, from Miyamoto Shrine, http://www.miyamotoshrine.com/theman/interviews/230403.shtml.

Montfort, N. 2003. *Twisty little passages: An approach to interactive fiction*. Cambridge, MA: MIT Press.

Myers, D. 1984. The pattern of player-game relationships. *Simulation & Games* 15:159–85.

Myers, D. 1990. A Q-study of computer game players. *Simulation & Gaming* 21:375–96.

Myers, D. 1991. Computer game semiotics. *Play & Culture* 4:334–45.

Myers, D. 1992. Time, symbol manipulation, and computer games. *Play & Culture* 5:441–57.

Myers, D. 1999. Simulation, gaming, and the simulative. *Simulation & Gaming* 30:482–89.

Myers, D. 2003. *The nature of computer games: Play as semiosis*. New York: Peter Lang.

Myers, D. 2005. /hide: The aesthetic of group and solo play. Retrieved January 1, 2009, from DiGRA 2005, Changing Views: Worlds in Play. http://www.digra.org/dl/db/06276.04321.pdf.

Myers, D. 2007. Self and selfishness in online social play. In Akira Baba, ed., *Situated Play, Digital Games Research Association Conference Proceedings*, 226–34. Tokyo: University of Tokyo.

Myers, D. 2008. Play and punishment: The sad and curious case of Twixt. In *The*

[Player] Conference Proceedings, 275–301. Copenhagen: IT University of Copenhagen.

Myers, D. 2009. Forms of rules of games of forms. In J. Sorge & J. Venus, eds., *Erzählformen im computerspiel: Zur medienmorphologie digitaler spiele.* Bielefield: Transcript.

Myerson, R. B. 1999. Nash equilibrium and the history of economic theory. *Journal of Economic Literature* 37 (3): 1067–82.

Nieuwdorp, E. 2005. *The pervasive interface: Tracing the magic circle.* Retrieved January 1, 2009, from DiGRA 2005, Changing Views: Worlds in Play. http://www.digra.org/dl/db/06278.53356.pdf.

Orland, K. n.d. Originality, or "Where's the story, Nintendo?" Retrieved January 1, 2009, from Super Mario Bros. Headquarters, http://www.smbhq.com/rants/rant9.htm.

Papert, S. 1993. *Mindstorms: Children, computers, and powerful ideas.* 2nd ed. New York: Basic Books.

Palo Alto Research Center. 2005. *Grouping ratio by class and level.* June 16. Retrieved January 1, 2009, from Play on: Exploring the social dimensions of virtual worlds, http://blogs.parc.com/playon/ archives/2005/06/grouping_ratio.html.

Parsons, T. 1937. *Structure of social action.* New York: McGraw-Hill.

Pellis, S., & A. Iwaniuk. 1999. The problem of adult play fighting: A comparative analysis of play and courtship in primates. *Ethology* 105 (9): 785–806.

Pellis, S., & V. Pellis. 1998. The structure-function interface in the analysis of play fighting. In M. Bekoff & J. A. Byers, eds., *Animal play: Evolutionary, comparative, and ecological perspectives,* 115–40. Cambridge: Cambridge University Press.

Piaget, J. 1932. *The moral judgment of the child.* London: Routledge & Kegan Paul.

Piaget, J. 1954. *The construction of reality in the child.* New York: Basic Books.

Piattelli-Palmarini, M. 1994. *Inevitable illusions: How mistakes of reason rule our minds.* New York: John Wiley & Sons.

Poblocki, K. 2002. Becoming-state: The bio-cultural imperialism of Sid Meier's *Civilization. Focaal—European Journal of Anthropology* 39:163–77.

Postman, N. 1986. *Amusing ourselves to death: Public discourse in the age of show business.* New York: Penguin Books.

Raessens, J., & J. Goldstein, eds. 2005. *Handbook of computer game studies.* Cambridge, MA: MIT Press.

Rafaeli, S., & F. Sudweeks. 1997. Networked interactivity. *Journal of Computer-Mediated Communication* 2 (4), http://jcmc.indiana.edu/vol2/issue4/rafaeli.sudweeks.html.

Rascaroli, L. 2002. *Like a dream: A critical history of the oneiric metaphor in film theory.* Fall. Retrieved from *Kinema,* http://www.kinema.uwaterloo.ca/rasc022.htm.

Reynolds, B. 1996. Designer's notes. In Sid Meier's Civilization II: *Instruction Manual,* 179–83. Hunt Valley, MD: Micropose.

Rheingold, H. 2000. *The virtual community: Homesteading on the electronic frontier.* Cambridge MA: MIT Press.

Ricoeur, P. 1981. *Hermeneutics and the human sciences: Essays on language, action, and interpretation.* Trans. J. B. Thompson. Cambridge: Cambridge University Press.

Rodriguez, A. M., & M. J. Egenhofer. 1997. Image-schemata-based spatial inferences: The container-surface algebra. In S. Hirtle & A. Frank, eds., *Lecture notes in computer science,* 1329:35–52. Laurel Highlands, PA: Springer-Verlag.

Rogers, A., R. K. Dash, S. D. Ramchurn, P. Vytelingum, & N. R. Jennings. 2007. Coordinating team players within a noisy iterated prisoner's dilemma tournament. *Theoretical Computer Science* 377:243–59.

Rojas, R. 1996. *Neural networks*. Berlin: Springer-Verlag.

Ryan, M.-L. 1992. *Possible worlds, artificial intelligence, and narrative theory*. Bloomington: Indiana University Press.

Salazar, J. 2005. *On the ontology of MMORPG beings: A theoretical model for research*. Retrieved January 1, 2009, from DiGRA 2005, Changing Views: Worlds in Play, http://www.digra.org/dl/db/06276.36443.pdf.

Salen, K., & E. Zimmerman. 2003. *Rules of play: Game design fundamentals*. Cambridge, MA: MIT Press.

Schechner, R. 1988. Playing. *Play & Culture* 1:3–19.

Schechner, R. 2002. *Performance studies*. New York: Routledge.

Scott, J. 2000. Rational choice theory. In G. Browning, A. Halcli, & F. Webster, eds., *Understanding contemporary society: Theories of the present*, 126–37. Thousand Oaks, CA: Sage.

Searle, J. 2002. Why I am not a property dualist. *Journal of Consciousness Studies* 9 (12): 57–64.

Seifert, U. 2008. The co-evolution of humans and machines: A paradox of interactivity. In U. Seifert, J. H. Kim, & A. Moore, eds., *Paradoxes of interactivity: Perspectives for media theory*, 8–23. Bielefeld: Transcript Verlag.

Sent, E.-M. 2004. Behavioral economics: How psychology made its (limited) way back into economics. *History of Political Economy* 36 (4): 735–60.

Shleifer, A. 2000. *Inefficient markets: An introduction to behavioral finance*. Oxford: Oxford University Press.

Sirlin, D. 2006. *Playing to win*, http://www.sirlin.net/ptw.

Skov, M., & O. Vartanian, eds. 2008. *Neuroaesthetics*. Amityville, NY: Baywood.

Smith, P. K., ed. 1984. *Play in animals and humans*. Oxford: Basil Blackwell.

Spariosu, M. 1989. *Dionysus reborn: Play and the aesthetic dimension in modern philosophical and scientific discourse*. Ithaca, NY: Cornell University Press.

Spariosu, M. 1997. *The wreath of wild olive: Play, liminality, and the study of literature*. Albany, NY: SUNY Press.

Spencer-Brown, G. 1972. *Laws of form*. New York: Julian.

Squire, K. 2002. Cultural framing of computer/video games. *Game Studies* 2 (1), http://gamestudies.org/0102/squire/.

Stephenson, W. 1999. *The microserfs are revolting:* Sid Meier's Civilization II. October. Retrieved January 1, 2009, from *Bad Subjects*, http://bad.eserver.org/issues/1999/45/stephenson.html.

Suber, P. 1990. *The paradoxes of self-amendment: A study of logic, law, ominipotence, and change*. New York: Peter Lang.

Sun, H. & C. T. Lin. 2005. *The "white-eyed" player culture. Grief play and construction of deviance in MMORPGs*. Retrieved January 1, 2009, from DiGRA 2005, Changing Views: Worlds in Play. http://www.digra.org/dl/db/06278.21161.pdf.

Sutton-Smith, B. 2001. *The ambiguity of play*. Cambridge, MA: Harvard University Press.

Tan, E. S. 1996. *Emotions and the structure of narrative film: Film as an emotion machine*. Mahwah, NJ: Lawrence Erlbaum Associates.

Taylor, T. L. 2006. *Play between worlds: Exploring online game culture*. Cambridge, MA: MIT Press.

Turner, V. 1969. *The ritual process: Structure and anti-structure.* Chicago: Aldine.

Turner, V. 1990. Are there universals of performance in myth, ritual, and drama? In R. Schechner & W. Appel, eds., *By means of performance: Intercultural studies of theatre and ritual*, 8–18. Cambridge: Cambridge University Press.

van den Belt, P. n.d. Civilization II: *One City Challenge Strategy Guide.* Retrieved January 18, 2004, from http://www.paulvdb.cistron.nl/occ/occ.htm.

Verenikina, I., P. Harris, & P. Lysaght. 2003. Child's play: Computer games, theories of play, and children's development. Retrieved August 1, 2009, from http://crpit.com/confpapers/CRPTV34Veren.kina.pdf.

Walther, B. K. 2004. *Cinematography and ludology: In search of a lucidography.* Retrieved January 1, 2009, from *dichtung-digital,* http://www.brown.edu/Research/dichtung-digital/2004/1/Walther/index.htm, 2004.

Ward, R. R. 1999. *Why DOOM was so good.* December 11. Retrieved January 1, 2009, from Trilobite.org, http://www.trilobite.org/doom/index.html.

Wellek, R. A. 1991. *History of modern criticism, 1750–1950.* Vol. 7, *German, Russian, and Eastern European criticism, 1900–1950.* New Haven, CT: Yale University Press.

Wimsatt, W. K., & M. Beardsley. 1954. *The verbal icon: Studies in the meaning of poetry.* Lexington: University of Kentucky Press.

INDEX